Crystals

Crystals

How to use their
healing powers

Emily Anderson

ARCTURUS

To my boys Jake and Ethan

Images courtesy of Shutterstock and Pixabay.

ARCTURUS

This edition published in 2021 by Arcturus Publishing Limited
26/27 Bickels Yard, 151–153 Bermondsey Street,
London SE1 3HA

ISBN: 978-1-3988-1321-2
AD007327US

Printed in China

Contents

Introduction 6

The Best Crystals For Meditation 16

The Best Crystals For Manifestation 44

The Best Crystals For Home Use 72

The Best Crystals For Healing 104

The Best Crystals For Divination 132

Index 159

Further reading 160

Introduction

Crystal healers believe the earth contains within it the wisdom to heal our modern ills. Stare a while at a sparkly geode of amethyst or handle a smooth, perfect pebble of jade and they claim you will not just see the beauty in the stone, but also sense the energy it is emitting.

It is thought that a well-placed crystal can help us boost the energy of a place, calm our children, and enable us to have a good night's sleep. Used for centuries all over the world for healing, psychic divination, decoration, and spiritual development, crystals have a timeless power and attraction.

Today we use them in water bottles, in healing treatments, and to counteract the effects of electromagnetic fields in modern life. These crystalline allies continue to capture our imaginations and give us tangible ways of connecting to the spiritual realms.

This book will show you how crystals can help ground you, energize you or open up your intuition. Placed in the right area of your home, they are believed to attract abundance, love or psychic powers. Through right intention, focus, positioning and belief, you can use crystals to create genuine magic in your life.

However, it should be said here that the ideas and suggestions in this book are within the spiritual realm and are not intended to be a substitute for conventional medical help. Always consult your doctor before undertaking any alternative therapy to ensure that there are no counter-indications for your health.

History of crystal use

Crystals have always been sought after by nobility, used in spell-work by witches and mystics, and held in high regard both aesthetically and energetically. Until medieval times, garments—especially those of soldiers and explorers—had empowering amulets woven into them while incantations were chanted, to keep the wearer safe from harm and help wounds heal quicker. During the Middle Ages, healing gems were placed on saints' shrines and given religious as well as magical powers. In St Paul's Cathedral, in London, the sapphire on St Erkinwald's shrine was said to cure any visitors' eye diseases.

Native Americans believed positive energies from gemstones could be passed from one species to another, crystal to human to animal, in what they called a sacred hoop or circle of existence. Such traditional societies believed crystals to be conscious. Their interactive, supportive energies were said to amplify and focus our innate healing and intuitive abilities.

Lapis lazuli used in an Eye of Horus design for a woman's necklace in Ancient Egypt.

The book of Genesis in the Old Testament has one of the earliest references to a healing stone, which belonged to Abraham. This stone was reported to immediately cure any sick person who looked at it. In the Papyrus Ebers, from about 2500BCE, the healing properties of certain gems are listed. Rubies are thought to help liver and spleen diseases, lapis lazuli was made into eye balm, while emeralds were used for curing dysentery.

Even Plato, the Greek philosopher who lived from 427 to 347BCE, talked of crystals as being made by the stars, and planets converting decayed material into the most perfect gemstones, which were then ruled by these planets. If the Sun was in a certain constellation or the moon or another planet ascending at the time of engraving a crystal, it would make it even more powerful. It's believed that stones, including moonstone and topaz, strengthen in power during a waxing moon (the time between a new and full moon, when the moon appears to be getting bigger), peaking in healing ability when the moon is full.

Ancient Egyptians, the Chinese and alchemists up until the 18th century added crushed crystals to medicines, believing strongly in the physical and medical healing properties of gems. Over 200 gems and crystals that could be used in healing were listed in the Greek pharmacist Dioscorides' *De Materia Medica*. And the first Roman chronicler, Pliny, includes older crystal teachings in his *Natural History* and elaborates on the theory that the size and substance of the special stones used were important in the healing of different diseases. Despite the demise of other forms of traditional medicine practices, crystal healing remained popular far longer.

Does size matter?

Many crystals have electromagnetic energy fields, making them like a magnet. It may be that the larger crystal transmits more energy, but a smaller crystal can emit energy just as effectively with the right conscious intent and focused direction, when you become expert at doing so. Working with smaller gemstones is simply more practical, especially when you want to lay them on the body, or wear or carry them as a magic talisman.

In a spacious home, you can have a large piece sitting in the corner of a room or you can dedicate a small windowsill as seen here—both are beautiful and powerful.

Most experts and practitioners agree that a crystal of any size, rough or smooth, has healing properties. Clearly, the ancients would only have used the rough gems found in caves, deep in the earth, whereas today you can easily buy sparkly, domed geodes or smaller gems tumbled

and polished into perfectly smooth shapes. You can get rose quartz in the shape of hearts, or clear quartz made into a pyramid. While a crystal wand, made into a point, directs energy better, a rough or smooth texture doesn't matter when it comes to the power of crystals.

Whatever the shape or size, the healing and transformative properties of the stone come from the crystal itself and not its size; it's about how you work with them. Using them with love and clear, positive intention magnifies the benefits of any stone. You just need to make sure they are as close to genuine natural crystals as possible, for there are many imitations around nowadays.

Crystals found in nature have flaws and unequal coloring. They change over time, fading, becoming cloudy or veined over years of use. These gems develop naturally deep in the Earth, in rivers or cliffs, over a long period of time without any intervention. Specific types of crystals are found in particular locations; for example, turquoise is found in desert areas and created when water interacts with rock containing copper, aluminum and phosphorus. It is quite rare, so usually very expensive. Don't be fooled into thinking less expensive howlite that has been dyed to look like turquoise is the real thing. Dyed gems can look obviously dyed, in too-bright colors, or more natural. Many stones, including agate, howlite, jasper, quartz, dalmatian stone, and granite are very often dyed to boost their visual appeal, without really taking away anything from their quality. Even in Pliny's *Natural History*, it is recorded that gems were boiled in honey to enhance their appearance. Most rubies and sapphires have been treated in some way to improve their color, and emeralds often have their fractures filled and clarity improved.

Synthetic gems can be found more and more. They're not strictly fakes, as they contain the same chemical properties of raw gems but are created in laboratories in a condensed amount of time, and often seem more vibrant or uniform in color. They're also cheaper, but won't hold quite the same quality of energy as natural stones formed over centuries by the earth.

Fake crystals are not made of the same materials at all. They can look too perfect and can be cast from plastic, resin, ceramic or even painted rocks, just designed to look the same as real crystals. If there are bubbles in the gem, it's likely to be glass. Other methods of imitating crystals are with composites, which take the real mineral and just use it to coat glass or another rock.

The best way to avoid anything but the genuine item is to buy from reputable crystal shops or trusted experts. Ask where the crystal you like is from and have a really good, close look at it. Check its appearance and, most importantly, how it feels to you.

Choosing your crystals or rather letting them choose you

Do some research online or in books, or just browse around some crystal shops, and you will find certain crystals attract you much more than others. These are the ones for you. If you find yourself picking one up and you can't put it down, purchase it if you can, as it fits perfectly with your needs and desires at this time.

Cleansing and charging your gems

Crystals naturally pick up energy from their surroundings and anyone who's handled them. So, before you use them, you need to cleanse them – and then again at least every month, more if you're using them for intense healing sessions – to keep them working at optimum power.

There are many different ways to cleanse a crystal, and some are very specific to each stone. Check first that your crystal won't be damaged by the method you choose; some are delicate and can disintegrate in salt water, for example, or fade in too much sunlight. Here are the main ways to cleanse crystals:

✦ If your crystal is hard, and not likely to be harmed by water, a quick way to cleanse it is to hold it under running water for a few minutes or immerse it in the sea or a river.

✦ Most crystals like to be charged by the full moon's light or sunlight. Leave your gems outside on the night of a full moon and the following day so they soak up a full night and day of bright moon and sunlight.

✦ Put your crystals in a pot of herbs generally used for healing

and purifying, such as rosemary, sage or lavender. A day immersed in any of these scented leaves or flowers will absorb any dense and unwanted energy.

✧ If you live near stone circles, ancient burial mounds or other sacred sites, take your crystal there straight after the sun rises and lay them out on a flat stone if possible. Leave them for at least half an hour, and the negative energies in the gems will soak into the stones, while the power from the area will empower them.

✧ Smudging—wafting the smoke from a special, cleansing bundle of sagebrush or cedar—is an ancient way of cleansing your energy and environment, and it works very well for crystals too. When you have your smudge stick gently smoking, simply pass each crystal through the purifying smoke a few times so the cleansing scent is absorbed.

✧ You can also buy special crystal cleansing sprays from shops specializing in alternative spirituality, and one drop or spray on each stone should do the trick.

Now that your crystals are cleansed, they are ready to be charged with your intention, whether that's to heal others, connect with your higher consciousness or manifest certain things in your life. To do this, simply ask your crystal to do what is needed for your personal or spiritual growth, and to always work for the highest good for all. Whatever your request from your gems might be, it's worth adding "this or something better" so that the outcome is left up to higher powers, and may even surprise you with its brilliance.

After working with a crystal for a specific purpose, thank it for its help if you've finished the work, or ask that it keep acting on your behalf, either when you use it again for the same purpose, or just while you go about your day.

The Best Crystals For Meditation

Meditating using crystals will deepen your meditation practice, increase your intuition, and help you to connect with higher consciousness, spirit guides, and even angels.

Meditating with crystals

Creating a daily meditation practice is incredibly beneficial. It brings peace, patience, clarity and relaxation. Add some crystals to that practice and you can develop your spirituality further—heightening your intuition, encouraging telepathy or communing with the angelic realm, spirit guides or your ancestors.

The following section lists ten of the best crystals to meditate with to expand your consciousness further than you dreamed possible. Find out which crystals resonate with you the most, or choose according to which psychic skills or mystical experience you'd most like to have. Maybe you'd like to try placing a crystal on each chakra for a full-body boost. See the section on page 34 to find out more.

GETTING STARTED

✧ Find somewhere quiet where you can be undisturbed and comfortable for ten to 20 minutes or more. Lie down on the floor, or sit upright on a pillow or a chair.

✧ Hold your chosen crystals in your hands. Feel their energy permeate your body and the space around you.

✧ Set an intention for the crystals in this meditation. Visualize those intentions in detail in your mind, and imagine this charging up your crystals with purpose to help you in whatever path you've chosen at this time. Continue holding the crystals in your hands, or you can place them on the chakras they clear and strengthen. Or simply place them by your side to work their magic beside you.

✧ Now, close your eyes and relax. As with all meditation, begin by focusing on your breathing. Allow yourself to take some nice deep breaths in, and some slow breaths out. Inhale. Exhale.

✧ Allow the energy of the crystal to have an effect—but don't force it or worry if it doesn't. Just continue relaxing and breathing deeply, and see what unfolds. You may get a strong sense to do something new in your life; you might hear messages from other beings; you could even have visions of past-life experiences. Just witness it all, knowing you are safe.

POWERFUL EFFECTS

✧ When you feel like you've come to the end of your meditation, count down from 10 to one to bring your awareness back into the room. Wriggle your fingers and toes, or stretch, keeping your eyes closed. Now, imagine your feet are like the roots of a tree going deep into the ground. Your body is strong and rooted to the earth. Hold this visualization for a few minutes to strongly ground your energy back into the present moment, necessary after traveling to other realms or being in a relaxed state of bliss for a while.

✧ When you're ready, move slowly from your position and go about your day. Have a notebook nearby to note down any experiences you had that resonate, or any questions that have arisen. You may find yourself having sudden realizations or epiphanies about issues in your life.

Keep meditating with your favorite crystals and you will gain a stronger sense of purpose in your life. You may connect with a particular spirit guide or angel who will help you on your path. Your dreams will probably become more vivid, with clear messages or symbolism that you remember easily on waking. Your ability to sense what's about to happen or what someone is going to say or do may be stronger. Your connection with others, your creativity and your destiny will become better than it has ever been. All because you took the time to simply be with some of the most powerful, life-changing tools on our planet.

Amethyst

BEST FOR:
Developing your spirituality, deepening meditation, and enhancing creativity.

LOOKS:
Pale lavender to deep purple quartz, sometimes opaque, sometimes transparent, with white or clear streaks.

Amethyst is one of the most spiritual stones, and has a very high vibration. Used by ancient royalty to encourage sobriety and spiritual grounding, this purple quartz will help you tap into a deeper, more centered, spirituality. It helps still the mind of mental chatter, calm anxieties, and inspire a deeper meditative state. This will enable you to really tune into your intuition, and it will also allow your psychic side to develop.

Add an amethyst geode to your meditation altar, where you can sit next to it and feel its powerful calming effects, removing any tension or stress in your life. Alternatively, lie down to meditate with a smaller stone placed on your third eye, as amethyst opens this and the crown chakras, further enhancing your psychic abilities.

To increase your awareness further in meditation, sit holding a single stone or small clusters in your left hand, with the point toward your left arm, to draw the calming spiritual energy into your body.

The ancient Egyptians made amulets from amethyst as a form of prayer and to protect against harm. It is still used today as a protection stone, to ward off psychic attack by creating a protective shield of light around the body.

Hold a sizable chunk in your left hand, resting on your right hand, while sitting comfortably and allowing your breath to deepen and your worries to melt away. Imagine the purple amethyst energy forming a protective light around your body as you travel safely into other worlds in your mind. Meditating in this way with an amethyst can also bring success and help you focus on new endeavors. Its ability to expand your higher mind means it can boost your creativity, imagination and passion for new projects.

A soothing stone, especially for children, it can help relieve insomnia and curb nightmares. Place it under your child's pillow to help them drift into a peaceful sleep. Or rub a point of amethyst counterclockwise in the center of the forehead to alleviate fear of the dark and recurring dreams.

Worth wearing as a pendant due to its powers of protection from negativity, it can also help soothe your spirit after the death of a loved one and bring your emotions back to balance after any disturbance.

Angelite

BEST FOR:
Communing with the angels, developing telepathy and clairvoyance, and for clear communication.

LOOKS:
White exterior with light blue inside.

Angelite is highly evolved celestite that has been compressed for millions of years to form nodules. It is made of calcium sulphate and found in Peru. This stone of awareness and tranquility helps soothe excessive emotions and create a deeper inner serenity. Vibrating at the frequency of benevolence, its energy can greatly assist during difficult times and guide you on your spiritual journey.

Sit next to, or hold, a piece of angelite crystal when you meditate to receive the love and guidance imbued in this rare gem. Feel the love and support that the angels can give you.

If you have a meditation altar, place a piece of angelite on it and let your gaze rest upon it, eyes half open. Tune into your angelic guides or guardians from the higher planes, bringing you their wisdom and guidance, in messages, symbols or general sensations. Meditate regularly using angelite to increase any psychic abilities, including channeling, clairvoyance, mediumship and spiritual healing.

Angelite is a helpful stone for astrologers and anyone involved in giving readings or spiritual counseling, as it encourages clear and balanced communication of insights. Have it beside you if you do any readings for others, to help you share messages from spirit guides, the stars or cards, with compassion and kindness.

Connected to the crown, third eye and throat chakras, it aligns them all, bringing you closer to the angelic realms. Wear it on a choker-style necklace to clear negativity from the throat chakra in particular, to help soften your speech and avoid rambling. Wearing it here can also help bring peace in relationship conflicts. Physically, it can help you with emotional overeating and healing broken bones when worn on the body or through crystal healing.

This gentle gem increases the spiritual nature of your dreams and helps you interpret their guidance correctly. It also assists with tuning into the Akashic records (where everything that has ever happened is recorded in the etheric realm) in your dreams. Place a piece of angelite next to your bed to help you stay lucid in dreams and remember the wisdom revealed in them when you wake up. Make sure you keep your angelite crystal dry. It's so delicate, it can be damaged by water.

Azurite

BEST FOR:
Connecting with the heavenly realm, reaching the quiet stillness at the heart of meditation, receiving healing and psychic experiences.

LOOKS:
Bright to deep blue and indigo, sometimes with light blue streaks.

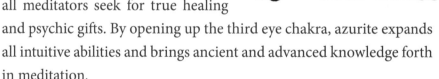

Known as the "stone of heaven" by the ancient Chinese, azurite connects our worldly realm to that of the gods, and to the void beyond all awareness that all meditators seek for true healing and psychic gifts. By opening up the third eye chakra, azurite expands all intuitive abilities and brings ancient and advanced knowledge forth in meditation.

It can enhance your dreams, take you into a channeling state and help you astral-travel safely. Elevating the powers of the mind, it can clear tension, confusion, and bring forth new perspectives, allowing you to envisage and manifest exciting possibilities in your life.

Azurite has been used to guide people to enlightenment ever since the earliest civilizations began. The Mayans used it to spark their mystical side, while Native Americans would meditate with it to contact their spirit guides and receive messages. In Atlantis and Ancient Egypt, it was only priests and priestesses who knew the full power of such a special psychic stone.

The potent energies in this gem are better released through touching, so hold a smoothed stone of azurite in your hands during meditation and ask for its help. It makes a great touchstone during a past-life regression session to journey successfully back to previous lives. Whether you wear it or carry it in your pocket, be sure to smooth your fingers over it often.

This stunning stone will inspire new interests and connections with others. It also encourages an aspiration for more knowledge and awareness. Place one on your desk to touch often and feel the invigorating, mind-expanding energies. Great to use when studying for a test, or thinking up new ideas for a project, it's believed to boost concentration and memory retention. It's definitely a stone to discreetly rub between your fingers during an interview or presentation to focus the mind. Azurite is a good crystal for the elderly to wear, or meditate with, to fortify their mental alertness and overall brain health.

This bright blue stone clears the throat chakra so the new ideas and experiences you've just received can be perfectly communicated. Wear it as a necklace or place it on the throat area when lying down in meditation. Its clairvoyant energy makes azurite perfect for a pendulum, for dowsing accurate and objective answers to questions.

Black Tourmaline

BEST FOR:

Protecting against negative thoughts, energies and radiation from electronics, also for grounding, easing panic attacks and motion sickness.

LOOKS:

Black or very deep blue-black, found in column structures.

Black tourmaline, also known as Schorl, is one of the most common crystals used in meditation due to its ability to keep you grounded. It connects the root chakra to the Earth's electromagnetic field, essential in these times of shifting energies on the planet.

This shamanic stone, used by ancient magicians when doing spellwork, provides a protective shield against any negative entities or bad vibes from people or places.

Known also as the "etheric bodyguard," it protects and purifies the etheric body, keeping you safe while you explore the spiritual realm. Place a smooth stone of black tourmaline in each hand or one in your left hand and a piece of selenite crystal in your right hand, to cleanse

your aura while you meditate.

Wear a black tourmaline brooch on your left side—where this crystal enters the aura—if you find yourself in unpleasant surroundings or mixing with angry, complaining or draining people.

Sit in meditation surrounded by a grid of black tourmaline stones to clear the mind of unwanted self-talk, cleanse the emotions and body of impurities, and rid the spirit of anything weighing you down. An essential crystal for anyone suffering from anxiety, depression or anger issues, try sleeping with some in your pillowcase to help clear you overnight.

If there's an area of your home where you feel more negativity, place a large piece of black tourmaline on its own there and let it transmute the energy around it. Working with black tourmaline promotes a sense of self-confidence and personal power.

Black tourmaline is believed to protect the body from harmful radiation and electromagnetic waves from gadgets such as computers and cell phones. Place a large piece of it next to any electrical device, or wear black tourmaline on your body when working on electrical devices for long periods of time.

Rub a piece of black tourmaline and it will become electrically charged, with one end positive and the other negative. It will then attract or repel dust particles, for example. It aligns the energy centers in your body to enable healing light to channel through you, increase physical vitality, and inspire a clear-headed and positive attitude.

Blue Calcite

BEST FOR:
Soothing wrought emotions, promoting inner peace. Helps with recuperation and clear communication.

LOOKS:
Opaque light blue and white.

The simplest forms of calcite are pure white, but other minerals in the compound create various colors, with light blue calcite being particularly soothing on the eye, the body and the emotions. If you need restoration and want to bring your life into balance, use blue calcite in meditation.

Its calming energy is beneficial for those suffering from anxiety, stress, or after a major life event. It releases negative emotions and encourages relaxation and healing. Sleeping with a chunk of blue calcite on your bedside table can work as a natural sedative, helping you drift off into a restful sleep, even after trauma or during times of mental anguish.

Blue calcite is a powerful purifier, and can be used to help absorb old behaviors or thought patterns and send back increased motivation and positive energy, transforming your life for the better. Meditating with blue calcite creates a more optimistic outlook by helping you see the perfection inherent in all of life.

Sit calmly, holding a blue calcite crystal in your hands, and say: *"I am connecting to a calming universal energy"* as many times as feels comforting, until you feel fully relaxed. In this state, your natural, creative side will manifest with new ideas and interests.

Place this soft blue gem on the third eye chakra while lying down meditating to activate strong intuition and inner vision. Blue calcite enhances the vividness of your dreams and helps you understand their symbolism. Because blue calcite also opens and strengthens the throat chakra, it will help you clearly communicate any insights you receive. Balancing this chakra can smooth relationship disagreements, enabling you to find new ways of looking at situations and resolve issues with others in a calm and patient way.

Being a powerful energy amplifier, blue calcite is also a good stone for distance healing. Send healing thoughts during meditation while holding a blue calcite crystal, and they are sure to reach the recipient.

Also known as the "stone of the mind," blue calcite increases memory and learning capabilities. Choose this stone to meditate with daily if you are studying, or in any academic field, as it will help you retain information more easily.

Blue Topaz

BEST FOR:

Peacefulness, truth, connecting with spiritual beings.

LOOKS:

Light blue transparent.

With its gentle frequency, blue topaz brings peace, helping to calm your emotions. Yet it also subtly energizes the mind, brings clarity and helps avoid procrastination. Wear a talisman of blue topaz to boost your self-confidence, increase your attention span and inspire creativity. If you need to think through complex problems or perfect your learning in some way, meditate with blue topaz before setting your mind to work with renewed dynamism.

Use blue topaz to connect with the spiritual realm and hear Divine wisdom clearly. Meditating with it will also enhance any affirmations and visualizations, and discern what is genuinely true for you. Sitting with blue topaz for some time will deepen your meditation practice and allow the physical body to assimilate wisdom from the higher mind. It will strengthen your inner guidance and improve your psychic abilities, making it a great gem to have by your side if you give readings to others.

When lying down to meditate, place a blue topaz stone on the throat or third eye chakra to help you make clear distinctions between what you would like or not like in your life. This will also enable you to consciously articulate any feelings and thoughts you want to express with regards to your personal desires.

Traditionally a gem of love and abundance, blue topaz can support you emotionally so you feel ready to receive affection from wherever it manifests. It's a soothing crystal to help you relax on all levels, enhancing and quickening spiritual development where it may have been blocked, and helping manifest your dreams.

The gentle blue color of this crystal can help you see your truth, and will highlight any behavior pattern or blueprint you've been following that has kept you from fully being your true self. It will cleanse the aura, encourage forgiveness, and disconnect you from any doubts you have about which path to take. Wearing this gem will connect you more to your higher consciousness, so it can lead you to your genuine aspirations.

Blue topaz can help you see the bigger picture of a situation as well as the details. Set goals while sitting quietly with blue topaz by imagining how they will play out on both a small and large scale in your life. Then fill your crystal with that creative, can-do energy and trust that the good things will unfold naturally while you allow yourself to just "be."

WHICH CRYSTALS FOR WHICH CHAKRAS?

Choose the right crystal for each of your chakras—the energy centers that run up and down your body—and you can balance and strengthen your whole system. Each chakra has specific stones that work best with it, so choose the one that resonates with you the most. Place each one onto the specific chakra while lying down, let your breathing and body relax, and the crystals will do the rest.

CROWN
Top of head: spirituality,
reaching higher dimensions, pure bliss
AMETHYST, CLEAR QUARTZ, SELENITE

THIRD EYE
Between the eyebrows: strengthens intuition, imagination,
decision-making and sense of purpose
AMETHYST, BLACK OBSIDIAN, BLUE CALCITE

THROAT
Center of neck: clear communication,
expressing your truth and feelings
BLUE CALCITE, BLUE TOPAZ, LAPIS LAZULI,
AQUAMARINE, TURQUOISE

HEART
Center of chest: self-acceptance,
love, joy, inner peace, trust
ROSE QUARTZ, JADE, MOLDAVITE

SOLAR PLEXUS
Two inches above belly button: enhances creativity,
confidence, personal power
MALACHITE, CALCITE, TOPAZ, CITRINE

SACRAL
Two inches below belly button:
sense of pleasure, sexuality and abundance
CITRINE, CARNELIAN, MOONSTONE

ROOT
Base of spine: helps you feel grounded,
balanced and independent
TIGER'S EYE, BLACK TOURMALINE, HEMATITE

Clear Quartz

BEST FOR:

Amplifying energy, raising your vibration, enhancing intuition and psychic ability.

LOOKS:

Clear crystal, shimmery in the light.

The most common yet most powerful mineral on earth, clear quartz is known as the "master healer," and was key to the development of many ancient civilizations. A staple spiritual and magical tool for Celts, Mayans, Aztecs, Egyptians and Native Americans, many believed these stones to be alive, incarnations of the Divine. They were believed to have a great power for healing and for raising consciousness.

Clear quartz magnifies the power of any other crystal as well as the body's natural energy, making it an essential stone for meditation and healing. While it stimulates the whole chakra system, it is especially good for opening the crown chakra. Regularly meditating with clear quartz will help expand your consciousness, connect with the angelic realm or remember past lives. Sleep next to some clear quartz and let its mesmerizing quality help you drift into a deep sleep, full of memorable and meaningful dreams.

Sitting quietly, place a quartz crystal on the heart chakra will transform any emotional blocks into self-acceptance and love. Placed on the third eye during meditation, clear quartz will increase mental clarity, filter out distractions and enable you to focus on the pure bliss of stillness beyond. Here, your intuition and psychic abilities can manifest.

Program clear quartz with your intention for your meditation, such as to connect with your spirit guides, and it will assist with this every time you use it.

Achieve any goal by sending the feeling of the desired result into the quartz during meditation. It will remember and magnify that energy, bringing forth opportunities for that outcome to manifest the more you meditate with it.

Clear quartz is used a lot in technology including watches, radio transmitters and receivers and memory chips in computers because it can store, amplify and transform energy. Place this healing gem on your desk if you work with computers or other electronic devices, as it repels the harmful effects of radiation from such equipment. Clear quartz also cleanses and protects the aura by removing positive ions and producing negative ions instead.

Because it's such an enhancer of energies, make sure you cleanse your clear quartz regularly in one of a variety of ways. You can soak it in a saltwater solution overnight, leave it in the sunshine, or smudge it with sage smoke.

Labradorite

BEST FOR:

Magic, protection, courage, traveling between realms.

LOOKS:

Gray, murky green, black, or grayish white with a rainbow of colored layers from bright blue and pale green, flashes of gold and coppery red.

Discovered in Labrador, Canada in 1770, labradorite's mystical and magical powers are mind-blowing. Looking like the Aurora Borealis—where the Inuit people believe the crystal came from—its "labradorescence" of colors flashes out of its mostly gray exterior. Underneath what appears to be a fairly ordinary stone is an array of reflective, spectral colors, symbolic of labradorite's ability to allow spiritual seekers and shamen to move through the dark, unseen realms while still keeping their own light strong.

Known as a "stone of magic," it's the go-to crystal for healers, magicians, and anyone who wants transformation, self-discovery and spiritual adventure. It helps with spirit communication, accessing Akashic records and understanding past lives.

Labradorite acts as a protective talisman for those who travel between worlds seeking knowledge and guidance, ensuring their soul

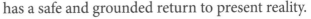

has a safe and grounded return to present reality.

Wearing or carrying labradorite allows your natural magical powers to surface, as well as bringing forgotten memories to light to help you move on from them. Meditating with it will awaken innate psychic abilities, such as telepathy, clairvoyance and awareness of synchronicity.

Amplify this stone's protection energy when journeying in meditation by imagining it transforming your body into a magical rainbow body shining with hues of blue, green, purple, violet and gold. Ask labradorite to activate this array of color within you, keep your vibration high and open all chakras.

You must use this crystal with intentions of developing a higher awareness, as labradorite wants you to expand your knowledge of both the light and the dark. Also known as the "stone of balance," it will help you face your darker, subconscious self and balance the two extremes within you, enabling you to shine even brighter after traveling inward.

Labradorite is most potent during dusk and dawn, when nature displays a similar spectrum of color and you can feel its energy more. Sit outside in the changing light, and see all humanity as one "being of light" transcending limitations of the past, and fears for the future, to see the infinite possibilities in the now. Part of this pure light, you can allow yourself to just "be."

Moldavite

BEST FOR:
Powerful transformation, healing, protection.

LOOKS:
Deep, forest green, olive, greenish brown and glassy, with carved, etched or wrinkled patterns in raw unpolished stones.

Found only in the Czech Republic, moldavite has extraterrestrial connections. It was created when a meteor crashed into the earth nearly 15 million years ago in the Bohemian Plateau, where pieces are scattered throughout the area. The shapes of moldavite found back up its molten origins: most are round to very flat, drop-like or disc shapes, spheres, ovals or spirals—all common liquid splash patterns.

Once as prized as emerald, its usage goes back to the Neolithic people of Eastern Europe, in 25,000BCE. They used it not only for arrowheads and cutting tools, but also as an amulet for protection, good fortune and fertility. It was found in the archaeological site of the Venus of Willendorf, the oldest known Goddess statue. A powerful addition to any meditation session, moldavite is an energy amplifier that opens up all the chakras, enhancing spiritual growth. Called a "stone of connectivity," connecting universal and earthly energies, it increases connection to intuition, telepathy and guidance from spiritual realms.

Meditating with this gem regularly will ease doubts and worries, especially about money, giving you insights into new solutions to any problems and helping you tap into the magic of the universe.

Moldavite has an intense vibration, often felt quickly and dramatically, that can take some getting used to. The first time you hold moldavite, it can feel warm to the touch, a feeling first felt in the hand and then through the body. It activates the heart chakra, felt as a pounding pulse, sweating or flushing of the face, and encourages cathartic release of outdated beliefs and ideas that no longer serve you. Let the tears or laughter flow, and know this crystal will help the heart and mind work together to change your life for the better.

Carrying a piece of moldavite or wearing it as jewelry will rejuvenate you and slow down aging. Vibrating at this heightened frequency means more beneficial synchronicities will come your way to help you transform and heal. But get used to wearing it slowly and take your time, as it can lead to light-headedness.

If you sometimes find it hard living on this planet, with its heavy energy, suffering and wild emotions, lie down with a piece of moldavite on your heart area. It will help you know the reasons why you are incarnated here at this time and give you a renewed sense of purpose and fulfillment.

Selenite

BEST FOR:
Deep connection to higher realms, improving telepathy and psychic insight.

LOOKS:
Pure white or translucent, grows naturally in wands, sometimes in pairs.

Selenite is named after the Greek Moon Goddess Selene and, much like the moon, represents tranquility, blessings and heavenly light. A stone for females—mothers in particular—it boosts libido, fertility and fidelity. It encourages commitment, communication between couples and helps you see through deception.

Naturally found growing in long, slender wands, selenite has a high vibration that activates the crown chakra, helping you connect with ancestors, angels and ascended masters. Meditating often with selenite will bring a deep peace, boost your telepathic and psychic skills, and protect your aura.

A selenite wand is a great tool for directing your intention and energy outward to others or the wider world, in prayer or manifestation exercises. Selenite wands are also used to sense energy blocks in the chakras and then send the crystal's pure light to clear the channel.

You can also create energy grids at home or outside with these wands. Lying in the center of a selenite grid means nothing negative will come to you, and you can experience true spiritual ascension.

When activating your selenite, try gently stroking it. To receive psychic insight, lie in meditation with a wand on the heart chakra pointing at your head and another on the floor with the point just touching your crown chakra. Breathe deeply and feel the calm clarity this crystal brings. In your mind, you may meet spiritual beings with messages for you, or receive visual symbols or stories about past lives or the future.

Alternatively, sit upright, breathing in deeply and imagining white light filling your body, allowing yourself to relax. Hold your selenite in your left hand and place your right hand underneath the left, cradling your crystal in your lap. Look gently at your selenite and attune yourself to its pure white light.

Next, slowly place your crystal on top of your head (the crown chakra) and let the white light of the selenite enter the crown. Move the gem to your third eye chakra and hold it there for a few minutes. Know that you are safe, and let your mind journey where it wants—to familiar places, through the stars, or channeling beings from other dimensions. Don't forget to ground yourself after communing with the cosmos. While selenite can be cleansed in water that the full moonlight has shone into, never leave it in water, as it will dissolve.

The Best Crystals For Manifestation

Whether you want a new job, more money or better relationships, use crystals to help you manifest the life you want.

Manifesting your desires

If you want to be more successful in your career, find a new partner or experience better health, then try manifesting with certain crystals.

Working with crystals will help you uncover and release any emotional blocks and challenges to the natural flow of abundance. Take time to meditate with the right one to focus inward, to discover what's stopping you from realizing your purpose and reaching your full potential. Perhaps it's fear, pain, sadness or exhaustion built up by past events and experiences, weighing heavy on your spirit. Take time to be kind to yourself and know that these feelings shall pass in time.

Remember to be grateful for all you already have. There is always something you can focus on in your present to be thankful for—a healthy body, a warm, safe home. Feeling gratitude for our life increases the flow of positive energy, bringing more wonderful things our way.

Meditating with crystals will bring clarity on what you really want in life, what changes you need to make to increase your luck and prosperity. They will connect with, cleanse and open up certain chakras to boost your energy and help attract the perfect situations and opportunities to you. Hold your chosen crystal while you meditate, or place it over its corresponding chakra to really feel the benefits of its stirring and proactive boost.

Manifestation is all about right timing and trusting that everything will work out as it's meant to, if you are open to the magic of the universe. Try setting an intention with a positive affirmation—charging a crystal to work for you. Imagine your life working out the way you want it to, and send that visualization into the crystal. Keep that charged crystal near you when you're working, or place it in your wallet to attract wealth and balance your spending.

Try wearing your charged crystal as part of a necklace, set in a ring, brooch or earrings to stay in contact with its powerful manifesting energy all day long. This will empower you to make the right decisions to lead you on the right path, and to know that you do deserve the things you desire.

Whichever way you decide to harness the power of crystals, they will bring you renewed confidence, positivity and insight to help you move forward toward the life of your dreams.

Citrine

BEST FOR:
Enhancing career, creativity and communication, manifesting abundance.

LOOKS:
Pale yellow to amber and orange quartz.

Citrine is also called the sun stone, and holds the clear energy of the morning sunlight, bringing joy, abundance and optimism to all areas of life, especially career and finances.

Historically known as "the Merchant's Stone," and associated with the planet Mercury, citrine is believed to improve a person's sales talk, upping their wealth and success in business. Long ago, merchants placed this stone in their vaults to protect their money and attract more. Today, businesses can get a boost by placing a small piece of citrine by the cash register or computer, if that's where the money is made, to help boost income.

Citrine is also known to encourage wise spending decisions by strengthening intuition. It allows you to release past anger, fears of lack and destructive habits blocking abundance, and encourages you to see a brighter future ahead. This boosts self-esteem and helps you enjoy new things, leading you to create and act on new opportunities for more prosperity.

Try this ritual for extra prosperity:

At dawn, burn a yellow candle next to a piece of citrine. This will charge the stone with abundance energies. Once the candle is burned down, keep the fully charged crystal in your wallet to attract wealth.

A powerful stone for anyone involved in communications or expressive arts, citrine ignites creative imagination and willpower by opening up the sacral chakra. Activating your imagination is the first step toward manifestation, because you need to first envision the future you want to bring it into being.

Visualize and really feel your desire becoming reality while holding a piece of citrine in your dominant hand. Imagine this vision charging the stone with energy to help you put plans into action to make it all come into being.

From the sacral chakra, citrine's energy wakes up the solar plexus and the root chakra, helping all three to radiate the stone's sunlight. This ignites our will and energy to work hard and persevere to make things happen out of the ideas coming from the imagination.

Citrine transmutes rather than absorbs negativity, so it never needs to be cleansed. But to enhance its radiance, leave citrine in sunlight from dawn until midday, especially on the summer solstice. Just don't leave it in direct sunlight too often, as it can fade or crack.

Golden Topaz

BEST FOR:
Amplifying and manifesting spiritual intention, giving courage, wisdom and success.

LOOKS:
Golden yellow silicate, although topaz forms in yellow, gold, orange, red, blue, green, purple and brown.

Also known as imperial topaz, this golden gem is associated with opulence, luxury and generosity. Topaz means "fire" in Sanskrit, and this crystal harnesses the fire of the sun to radiate a gentle energy with a powerful pull. Traditionally worn as a charm to attract a wealthy lover, now it's more of a spiritually rich soul-mate magnet in love rituals, while also used as a talisman to attract money and prosperity. Hope to manifest true love and friendship, the right person at the right time to help boost career, plus courage, charisma and success when working with golden topaz. This crystal reaches greatest power as the moon waxes to full moon.

Topaz is a "crystal of potency," because it produces linked negative and positive currents that transmit attraction and manifestation to the ether. Request your desires to the universe and embed them into this crystal with your mind, and you'll receive clarity and focus on the path to take to reach those goals. Topaz is one of the best gems to empower you with positive affirmations and bring clear visualization of the future in meditation.

With its golden shimmer, Topaz lifts the spirits, helps you feel better about yourself and gives you the energy to turn ideas and intentions into action. It clears away fatigue and outdated emotions or habits weighing you down, and replaces this with peace and well-being. Topaz activates the root, sacral and solar plexus chakras, as well as the crown, which increases your likelihood of transforming your highest path into action and making it reality.

Sit quietly and tune into your topaz to connect consciously to the heavenly realm and receive divine guidance, letting that wisdom be stored in the gem for future manifestation. It will recharge you physically and spiritually, boosting your faith in what's to come, increasing your confidence and pride in your abilities while remaining open-hearted and generous. Anyone in public speaking, teaching, sales or philanthropy would benefit from carrying a piece of topaz with them or wearing it on a pendant, to ensure that they speak the truth with kindness and love.

Topaz is also known as the "gourmet's stone," because it increases sensitivity to taste and stimulates the taste buds. Sucking on a piece of topaz before a meal or wine can help you appreciate it even more.

Golden or Gold Sheen Obsidian

BEST FOR:

Boosting personal power, spiritual manifestation and earth healing.

LOOKS:

Dark brown or black obsidian filled with a golden metallic sheen or sparkly gold "cat's-eye" effect in bright light.

Obsidian, usually dark brown or black, is nature's glass, formed from volcanic lava hardened so fast no crystalline structure is formed. It's also called "volcano glass," "mirror of the Incas," and "Iceland agate." This golden kind of obsidian has a shimmery "chatoyancy," or cat's-eye effect, that can be seen in strong light and was created by the alignment of gas bubbles during its formation.

This gem connects to the root and especially solar plexus chakras, working here to highlight and clear any persistent, long-term negative feelings that have to do with conflicts of ego or abuse of power. If you ever feel cynical about life, this crystal will help you get over such despondency, caused by past unpleasant events or traumatic experiences. It's a grounded and protective gem to help you clear emotional blockages, and then get motivated to move forward again.

Before manifesting anything, sleep with golden obsidian under your pillow to help alleviate any anxiety or stress. Then meditate with it to get clear about what's holding you back from manifesting your desires. Allow the crystal's energy to purify your energy field of any negativity. See its golden light permeating your solar plexus and root chakras, and fill your whole body and aura with its illuminating power.

Once beliefs and habits that no longer serve you are cleared away, the opportunity for new experiences can come into your life. Wear golden obsidian to help focus on what you want and how to manifest it over time.

Golden obsidian is good to gaze into and see the future, as well as for getting to the heart of a problem in the present. As well as diagnosing psychological issues for healing, golden obsidian helps with earth healing, pinpointing the place of disruption in the earth's energy system. Reiki practitioners, shamen or those working in the healing arts choose golden obsidian to help highlight and focus on the spiritual and physical places that need healing.

This strong stone helps you tap into your personal power and aligns it with higher consciousness. Allow golden obsidian to influence you, and it may reveal hidden talents and your true purpose in life.

Green Aventurine

BEST FOR:

Creating opportunities, good luck and prosperity.

LOOKS:

Light to mid green, opaque, oxide quartz often containing bright inclusions of mica, giving it a metallic glisten, especially when polished.

Aventurine is usually green, but also forms in blue, red, reddish brown, orange, peach, yellow, silver gray or dusty purple. Its name comes from the Italian word for chance, and refers to an accidental sparkly inclusion into glass in the 1700s. This name was then later given to the natural stone with its bright shimmer caused by mica particles in the quartz.

Known as the "stone of opportunity," green aventurine is the crystal to have with you if you need some good luck—whether in a job interview, on a first date, or trying your luck in a casino.

It's believed to line up opportunities for the taking, helping you manifest wealth and prosperity. Meditate with green aventurine and you'll be given visions and insights into how you can be lucky and achieve your goals through hard work and determination. This in turn brings positivity and boosts self-esteem so you know you deserve the best people, things and opportunities in your life.

Green aventurine rebalances the heart chakra, helping you to better understand your needs and feel what your heart really wants to manifest. It clears away any heartache and emotional blockages caused by mistakes or setbacks, and releases harmful behavior patterns. It's a great comfort crystal in times of change, giving you faith that you'll get through anything, enabling you to see tough times as a chance for growth and to build resilience, trusting in the greater good.

Its soothing energy can calm anger and nervousness, get rid of everyday stresses and harmonize erratic emotions. By bringing you back into balance, you can better manifest what you want, from a place of well-being. By working often with green aventurine in your manifestation rituals, you become a leader in your life, with improved decision-making abilities, motivation and belief in your own talents.

With the help of aventurine giving you a renewed zest for life, you can create better luck and move forward with confidence that good things will happen. It will help you see that the positive energy you put out in the world comes back to you, which is what manifesting good outcomes is all about.

Cleanse green aventurine often, as it absorbs negative energy. Place it outside, buried in the earth a few inches deep, to fully recharge.

Green Jade

BEST FOR:
Healing the heart to attract love and friendship, balancing mind, body and spirit, calmly and confidently acting on your dreams.

LOOKS:
Dark green and glassy or lighter, dull and waxy depending on whether it's nephrite or jadeite.

Jade is the name given to two different minerals: glassy-looking nephrite, a calcium magnesium silicate, and jadeite, a sodium aluminum silicate with a waxier veneer. The best way to tell them apart is by tapping with a hard object: nephrite will chime a musical note, jadeite won't. But they both help protect your finances and attract more wealth.

Since ancient times, green jade has been used to bring wisdom, abundance and prosperity. It helps you gets rid of negativity and see yourself as you really are, full of loving potential. It soothes irritability, stops damaging self-talk and ends self-imposed limitations blocking abundance. This gem brings the mind, body and spirit into balance, enabling manifestation to happen more easily.

Green jade connects with your inner child, bringing purity, joy and spontaneity, from which all good ideas and creativity manifest. It gives you confidence, self-esteem and self-reliance.

At work, place some green jade on your desk to boost success, especially when trying to attract new business or negotiate a deal. If people are confusing you with facts or figures, jade will keep your mind sharp to discern the best outcome. It will stimulate new ideas and make tasks easier to undertake. Rub a small, smooth stone of green jade to bring calm if you're dealing with difficult situations or overwhelmed with daily events.

This revered crystal is a powerful heart healer, softening and balancing any upset. Hold it to your heart center and you will feel its strong energies pulsing out through your whole body. Let it heal your heart, replenish your soul and support your spirit to move forward with love. Use this renewed energy to help you cherish your ambitions and make these desires reality.

Jade is the sacred stone of the New Zealand Maoris, who call it greenstone. Seen as a "dream stone," green jade can help encourage meaningful dreams. Position it on the forehead in meditation or before going to sleep to enable you to remember and understand the messages in your dreams, as well as release the suppressed emotions they represent.

Let this crystal remind you that we are all spiritual beings on a journey doing our best. Wear a green jade pendant every day to help you become more of who you really are, living from the heart, in each and every moment.

Peridot

BEST FOR:
Finding your purpose, attracting money, luck, peace and love, boosting well-being.

LOOKS:
Various shades of olive green, from light to the most prized dark olive green.

Our ancestors correctly believed that Peridot was brought to earth by an explosion of the sun, so carries the power of sunshine. The Ancient Greeks felt this gem exuded a vibration of royalty, bringing the wearer better health and increased wealth. They would carve the image of a torch onto a piece of peridot to encourage the manifestation of good fortune.

This crystal represents well-being and brings peace, warmth and radiance, reinvigorating mind and body to open up to new levels of awareness. It will connect you to divine consciousness, help you grow spiritually and realize your deeper purpose.

Meditate with peridot to bring understanding and insight into your self-sabotaging habits or the negative emotions holding you back. Stay connected to this crystal to realize your true worth, ultimate perfection and feel love, acceptance and gratitude—keys to manifesting the life you want.

Peridot powerfully generates the frequency of increase. Worn as jewelry, you can expect to manifest greater wealth, happiness and love in your life. Add it to a necklace as a pendant, and positive energy will flow from your heart space, increasing your awareness of love. If you wear peridot as a bracelet on your projective (right if you are right-handed) wrist, you'll easily share this loving energy with those around you. While having it on your receptive hand (the one you don't use that often—left if you're right-handed), you'll constantly be able to bring in more positivity, better health and increased prosperity.

Carry peridot in your pocket daily as a good-luck charm and to keep your energy high. At work or school, it can bring confidence in your talents, help you give an eloquent presentation and increase your profits. A protective stone, it will guard you from jealousy, deception and gossip.

It can give your love life a boost too—resolving heartbreak, releasing guilt or blame, and forgiving yourself and others, so you can move on in peace and happiness. It helps you feel content with your life, look inward for guidance and prize independence and acceptance.

Pyrite

BEST FOR:

Manifesting wealth, shifting from lack to abundance.

LOOKS:

Sparkly silvery gold, either in clusters or often in cubes.

Pyrite is famously called "Fool's Gold" after prospectors mistook it for real gold, long ago. It is actually a lighter color, harder and more brittle than real gold. Pyrite's shiny cubic composition will attract money to you when you work with it regularly.

Its name comes from the Greek word *pyr* or *pyros*, which means fire, because it creates sparks when struck with metal or stone. Consequently, it resonates with fire energy, bringing warmth, inspiration and confidence into your career and finances in particular. This stone awakens the inner warrior in us all, promoting strong will, focus and determination—needed to manifest the best in life.

This is a masculine stone of action and ambition, perfect for attracting more wealth and abundance. It connects with the solar plexus chakra and, when held there, sends a flood of power into this area to increase your zest for life. This helps you overcome any anxiety or destructive tendencies and build a solid foundation for new, more positive and productive habits to make you unstoppable in your achievements.

Work with pyrite in meditation as a mirror to yourself, letting it show you the causes behind, and solutions to, any feelings of unworthiness that will stop you from fully manifesting abundance. Hold some pyrite in your hand while looking at your reflection in a mirror. Gaze lovingly into your eyes and say, "I am worthy of success now."

Meditate with pyrite to stimulate your artistic energy and give you a creative edge if you work in the arts, architecture or sciences. Pyrite helps you commit to long-term projects, so it's an excellent stone for students to carry with them to their studies. It will also protect you from harm, especially if you're working or studying away from home.

Place a piece of pyrite where you work to bring high-frequency energy to the area, clearing stress caused by debts or working too hard. It will relieve mental confusion or fatigue and replace it with a clear head, renewed focus and enthusiasm. It can boost your leadership skills and give you the impetus to ask for and get a promotion. If you have a business card, place some pyrite on top of it to attract success and new career opportunities.

Rose Quartz

BEST FOR:

Manifesting unconditional love, romance and healing.

LOOKS:

Quartz with a rose-pink hue from traces of titanium, iron or manganese.

Rose quartz is known as "the love stone," and is said to have spread love, warmth and passion by legendary love god Cupid. This light-pink quartz brings peace and calm in relationships and melts away fear, resentment and anxiety, leaving you feeling carefree and open to love. The Egyptians believed in its healing abilities so much they carved rose quartz rocks into face masks believing it could clear the complexion and prevent the effects of aging.

Beads made of rose quartz have been found dating back to 7000BCE, from the civilization known as Mesopotamia, now Iraq.

Whether you want to increase your self-love, smooth over a family rift or bring a new lover into your life, rose quartz is a must-have crystal for your collection.

Thought to ease stress and induce rest, put a piece under your pillow at night, to help you get a good night's sleep and increase your love vibrations at the same time. Use it to open up your heart chakra and welcome love into your life. Lie down on your back in a comfortable place. Take a few deep breaths. Now place a small piece of rose quartz on the center of your chest, where your heart chakra sits. Breathe in its energy, imagining its soft pink hue filling your whole body with love. See this gentle pink energy of love clearing your heart chakra of any wounds from past relationships or your upbringing. Let it melt away any negativity from old partnership patterns. Keep breathing in that soothing, warm energy of love from the rose quartz as you go about your day.

Wear rose quartz as a pendant close to your heart chakra to open it up even more. Or carry a small tumbled rose quartz stone in your pocket all day to touch whenever you feel the need for some nurturing energy. Keep a chunk of rose quartz on your bedside table to keep the loving energy strong in your current relationship.

Set up a love altar in the love area of your home or bedroom to bring a loving relationship into your life. In feng shui, this is in the far right section of your room or floorplan. Place a rose quartz heart along with two red or pink candles to light daily, and meditate on true love coming into your life. Add other pairs of symbols of love—photos of happy couples or lovebirds—to the altar to boost your chances.

Tiger's Eye

BEST FOR:
Luck and bravery in new ventures, creative flow, willpower to stick with changes.

LOOKS:
Brown and golden silky stripes, in a "cat's-eye" effect.

Tiger's Eye is an ancient talisman said to bring good luck and great fortune. Ancient Egyptians believed it transmitted the power of the sun god Ra, while the Romans would carry this gem to battle to help them be brave. Thought to contain the power of not just the sun but the earth as well, tiger's eye helps transform pure energy into practical reality and tangible success.

It's a great stone to meditate with if you are planning a new project or taking up financial opportunities, as it will guide you to make balanced, rational decisions to bring success. Keep a piece of this crystal in your office or work area at home to manifest good fortune and attract a steady income, especially if you're an entrepreneur. It will help you stay focused on the task ahead and use your talents to maximum capability.

With its multi-dimensional access, tiger's eye can help if you need a fresh perspective, as it shows there are many ways to financial success.

Focusing on this gemstone will help you think outside the box and come up with interesting, creative solutions. If you have to present your ideas in a meeting, perform in public or take an exam, this bold gem will assist in overcoming any fears you have. It also brings wisdom to your spending, so when you manifest wealth you use it well.

If you want to manifest a healthier lifestyle, carry tiger's eye to boost your willpower and energy levels to help you stick with the changes you need to make. It is said to reduce cravings as well as feelings of inadequacy, and helps you persevere with the hard work of creating a healthy way of living.

Tiger's Eye can also help build better family relations. Having a prominent piece of it in the home will balance and soothe fraught relationships, encourage harmony and enable you to find common ground. It's one of the best gems to bring calm resolve to any crisis. Family counselors, professional mediators or anyone having to undertake tough negotiations should carry tiger's eye.

To make a prosperity charm with tiger's eye, keep a piece of it in a money pot and add a coin every day. Keep this pot in a warm spot to incubate wealth.

Titanium Rainbow Quartz

BEST FOR:

Awakening all chakras, creative expression, ultimate manifestation.

LOOKS:

Shimmery, rainbow-colored quartz.

Titanium Rainbow Quartz is quartz that has been specially bonded with titanium to give it its rainbow shimmer. This man-made gem is the most powerful of the coated quartz crystals, with titanium—otherwise known as the metal of power—greatly amplifying the effects of the "master healer" quartz. Consequently, this metallic stone is often called "the manifestation crystal."

This vibrant gem connects with, and energizes, the whole chakra system, sending Kundalini energy up the spine to boost your mood and help you realize and focus on what your soul needs for its evolution.

Creating a multi-dimensional shift in your life, it is said to awaken your innermost desires and parts of you formerly dormant so you can give more of your true self to the world. It will help you uncover your purpose, but if confusion or questions arise, wear titanium rainbow quartz around your neck in a pendant and the solutions will manifest.

With its rainbow shimmer symbolizing angelic guidance, wearing or carrying this stone will help you get in touch with this higher realm for inspiration and wisdom. This will heal your aura of any blockages holding you back from your full manifesting potential, and speed up whatever you want to come into being. As you connect with spiritual guidance more, meditating with this crystal will give you the confidence to communicate the messages you receive, and request back to the universe what it is you truly desire.

Also known as flame aura quartz, it can be an excellent muse, helping you find creative ways to express yourself. It will bring a sense of perfect timing to the things you say, and help you think clearly before speaking, so your words are taken in a positive way.

Place a cluster of titanium rainbow quartz on your desk at work for assistance when drafting emails or writing features or reports. If you have a novel in you, this crystal can help it manifest by inspiring you to get writing.

Let titanium rainbow quartz manifest more energy, humor and enjoyment in your life. This will enable you to relax and trust that your deepest dreams and desires will manifest into reality.

This gem is suitable for all astrological signs. It contains all the colors of the rainbow and stimulates all chakras.

Crystal recipes for manifesting

Here are some general tips on using crystals to manifest, plus specific combinations that work especially well.

- Choose any of the above crystals that resonate most with you or represent what you want to attract, and place them in a charm bag. Take your time holding and looking at each gem as you place it in the bag while stating its purpose or visualizing the outcome. Carry this charm bag with you to support you and bring your wishes to fruition.

- To manifest financial freedom and success, place a small bowl of money crystals from this section in the left-hand corner of your home or office as you stand from the front door. This is the money and career area according to feng shui. It should be free of clutter and contain pictures or ornaments that help you feel confident in your abilities and attract success.

✧ Add moldavite to titanium rainbow quartz for a power combo to transform you inside and out. Titanium quartz will have you pulsing with positivity, while moldavite will make you much more aware of the increased synchronicities that occur. They'll get you ready to act on them to move your life forward positively.

✧ To give your love life a lift, place crystals for manifesting love and romance, such as rose quartz, in the southwest corner of your home. Sleeping with some rose quartz under your bed or on your bedside table works in the same way to increase romance.

✧ Pair rose quartz with green aventurine to attract a new true love. Aphrodite, the goddess of love, is symbolized by rose quartz, while Tara, the goddess of the night, and Persephone, the spring goddess, add seduction and dynamism to green aventurine.

✧ Meditate with moonstone and rose quartz together, and they will align your chakras to make you positively glowing with divine charm, as well as awaken your intuition and make you aware of your deeper emotions, so you'll know if a new relationship is the one. This combination is also good for anyone in an established relationship, to keep it rooted in love.

✧ To manifest a family, place a rounded piece of amber with a pointed jet crystal in a red cloth bag tied with three knots of red ribbon. Put this fertility charm bag under the bed during lovemaking.

A crystal grid

Combining a few manifestation crystals in a grid makes them even more powerful, as their energies are combined with the sacred geometry of the formation you lay them out in, amplifying their ability to attract what you desire.

Print out or simply draw the seed of life geometry pattern representing the seven stages of creation. This sacred design represents the map to infinite possible paths and new beginnings, making it a great tool to focus your intention to manifest anything you want in your life. The symbol, combined with the crystals, will help you succeed at your goal in harmony, honesty and balance with your true intentions and what's ultimately right for you according to higher consciousness.

✧ First make sure the crystals you use have been cleansed and charged to connect with the energy of each other.

✧ Place strong amplifying and master attractor clear quartz in the center, then add these gems in positions that feel right to you.

✧ Iolite will reveal the mind and the heart's true desires, enhance your imagination to visualize what you want, and strongly attract your dream life to you.

✧ Some grounding and protective pyrite is good to have on your grid as a powerful crystal to manifest wealth.

✧ Add a piece of citrine to bring abundance and well-being.

✧ Good luck and prosperity gem jade needs to go on here, to gently open up your heart chakra to attract what your heart deeply desires.

As you're adding each crystal to the grid, really take the time to feel its frequency, and embed it with your intention to manifest a new lover, job or more money. Sit looking at the grid, and meditate on the crystals working to bring your desires to you at the right time. The most ideal time to create such a grid is a new moon; then, leave it out in your meditation area or on an altar for a lunar month to work its magic.

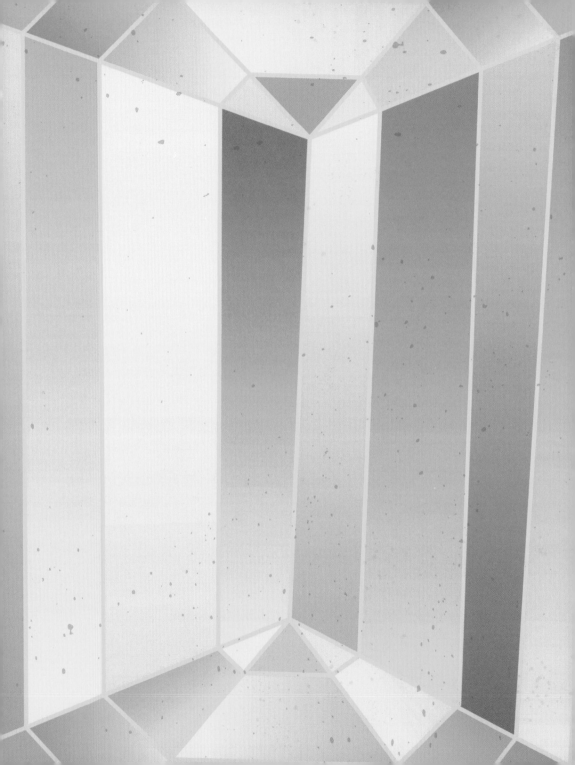

The Best Crystals For Your Home

Choose the right crystals for certain areas of your home and they will help protect you from harm, bring peace or energize where needed.

Crystals in the home

Having crystals in your home can only make you happier. Cleansed before use, programmed with conscious intention and positioned in the right place, they help in countless areas of your life.

Emotionally, they can clear the blockages and habits that are stopping you from living the life you want and deserve. Some, such as celestite and blue calcite, can lift your spirits, help you find your purpose, and get you to focus on making your goals a reality. Physically, gems can help calm you down, assist with healing, and block bad vibes. Spiritually, amethyst, peridot and clear quartz, among others, can enable you to meditate deeper, connect to higher dimensions and help you live in a new awakened, joyful way.

Certain crystals dotted around your home, workspace and yard will emit their energy into the areas they are positioned in. Blue lace agate is said to calm children, while a large piece of selenite in a house can generate a peaceful, positive atmosphere to smooth relationships. Other gems encourage organization, new romance, or help clear communication. They can also just make beautiful conversation pieces in the home, and can be dramatic additions to your decor.

A small bowl of your favorite crystals can keep the atmosphere in that room balanced and upbeat even if there's been drama, tension or change. It can encourage people to work together and not argue. Simple crystal tricks include keeping a piece of citrine in your wallet for increased wealth, or putting a piece of moss agate under your pet's

bed to help it settle down.

Gems will also work their magic according to feng shui, the ancient Chinese art of energy flow in the home. With this, your house or room is divided into different sections that reflect various areas of your life. For example, the left corner of your room is the career and wealth area, so you want gems such as citrine and jade there, creating dynamic and successful energy.

Crystals can also help our health by protecting us from the harmful effects of electromagnetic frequency and increased radiation from modern technology. Placing shungite, black tourmaline or smoky quartz between you and your device can soak up any potentially damaging energy.

Making crystal elixirs might work for you too. Simply leave your chosen crystal in a bottle of water in the fridge overnight to let its energies filter into the liquid. Then drink it when you need their energy, or make your guests cups of tea with it to pass on the good vibes.

In whatever way you want to use crystals in your home, surround yourself with the right amount. Choose intuitively, keep them cleansed, and ask them to work for you in the areas most needed.

Amber

BEST FOR:
Harmony and happiness in the home, attracting love, keeping calm.

LOOKS:
Mostly transparent golden, yellow or sometimes brown. Can contain fossilized insects or plants.

One of the world's oldest and most prized treasures, dating back between 30-60 million years in the Baltic, Amber is not actually a crystal but is fossilized resin from ancient coniferous trees. Because it sometimes contains plants or insects, it was said to contain the essence of life, and was seen as the stone of the mother goddess, connected to the sun and fire. It was used as a healing and protective amulet in Ancient Egypt, Cretan times (2000BCE), and the Middle Ages in Europe. Trade in this substance, reminiscent of the sun, created prehistoric trade routes in the world.

A protective charm, amber is a good gem to have in your home to attract prosperity as well as create an atmosphere of calm, cheerfulness and mutual respect. If it's new love you'd like in your life, wear it as a pendant. It connects with the solar plexus and sacral chakra to give you energy and motivation to act on your desires.

Brighten up your house with Amber's golden glow, and let its warm, sunny energy bring peace and stability to your home. It absorbs negative energy and transforms it into positive—and was once burned as incense for this purpose. A large piece of amber in the center of the room can dispel depression and anxiety, and boost self-worth so your inner radiance shines. Create a cozy cushioned area in your home where you can sit and look at a piece of glowing amber every day in winter to chase away seasonal affective disorder.

In a family home, Amber will help children relax, speak confidently and stay calm. It has been used for centuries to keep children from harm and ease teething pain. It also guards against conflict, again by taking the negative energy in the room and transforming it into positive.

Amber encourages the body to heal itself. Necessary in today's world, it can protect against electromagnetic pollution from technological gadgets, so place this crystal next to computers and phones. If you are sitting next to this substance while working, it will balance your own electromagnetic system and help get rid of headaches caused by stress.

Although usually golden orange, amber can also be blue, violet, green or black.

Black Obsidian

BEST FOR:

Protection, soaking up stress and negative vibes.

LOOKS:

Pure, glossy black or very dark brown.

Obsidian is made of earth, water and fire and formed from molten lava in the latter stages of volcanic eruptions. It was sharpened and used for tools and weapons as far back as 7,000 years ago. Obsidian is known as the mirror stone because it was once polished and used for mirrors and high-status decoration and scrying by the Mayans and other ancient civilizations. It's still a good tool for divination during meditation, as it can assist with seeing the future and contacting the spirit world.

Having obsidian in your home will make it a truly safe haven. Known as a "psychic vacuum cleaner," it clears negative energy from its environment. A protective stone, it will put up a barrier to burglaries or other unwanted guests, bullying from others, and psychic attack, enabling you to safely retreat from the world.

Its dark color is known to deepen your connection to the natural, physical world. Place a large piece on a table or wall in your yard or patio and allow obsidian to boost your strength and power, especially if you've felt drained or fearful about existence on earth during this tumultuous time.

Shiny black obsidian supports you in times of change, and blocks out everyday stresses and anxieties to help you relax. If you find you overspend, or overindulge in anything, an obsidian charm can boost self-control. However, it is also a powerful truth stone, and meditating with it will reveal your deepest insecurities and destructive patterns, which may not be easy to face, but when you're ready you can use black obsidian to help you heal your shadow side and become more balanced.

If you are finding obstacles to your career, place obsidian in the area of your home connected to career (the left-hand corner as you face inwards from the front door). A small sphere placed there, or a bowl of tumbled obsidian stones, will help rebalance your work energy, soak up stress, and inspire creativity so that your life can flow smoothly again.

Do not put obsidian on the floor, or anywhere it might get neglected, it needs to be regularly cleansed of all the negative energy it absorbs. Do this by placing it under any light source.

Blue Lace Agate

BEST FOR:

Creating a calm atmosphere, clear communication.

LOOKS:

Very pale blue with white or darker blue lines.

Blue lace agate, with its light-blue energy and slower frequency than many other crystals, will bring a calm, peaceful energy to any home. Sometimes associated with the Virgin Mary, and therefore motherhood, this gem nurtures and supports, soothes upset children, and helps healers increase their abilities.

Use this crystal at home or at work to diffuse anger and bring peace to any situation or gathering where there might be a clash of characters. Soak blue lace agate in bottles of water overnight to make an effective elixir for your family, friends or colleagues to drink. This will help avoid confrontations and ensure that criticism is expressed kindly.

Put some blue lace agate stones on your desk at work to transform any unhelpful, negative vibes with more uplifting, productive energy. Placed on a bedside table, the soothing, tranquil energy of blue lace agate will greatly relieve anxiety, stress or nervousness. It helps you find your voice and builds self-confidence to help you speak your truth with kindness. Wear it as a choker necklace to really work its magic on the throat chakra it corresponds with, opening and clearing it so your well-chosen words can flow freely.

Blue lace agate is also good for grounding and balancing the ups and the downs, the light and the dark, within us. If your siblings or children keep bickering, making you stressed and angry, light some blue candles surrounded by pieces of blue lace agate to bring serenity back to your home.

In feng shui, blue lace agate emits the still, strong and pure energy of water. This element brings rebirth and regeneration into your life. Add water's flowing and yielding yet powerful energies to the areas of your home where you feel it is most needed. Traditionally, the water element sits in the north of the home, the area associated with your life path and career. Place this crystal here and watch your career flow more smoothly. You can also put some of this crystal in the east side of your home for improved health, the southeast spot for abundance, and the southwest area to boost your love and marriage chances.

Celestite

BEST FOR:
Connecting to the angelic realm, calming atmospheres, soothing troubled relationships.

LOOKS:
Usually clusters and geodes of light blue, but can be found in white, orange, red and brown.

Celestite has a gentle, uplifting energy that cleanses its surrounding area, allowing you to relax and feel the presence of the celestial realm. This crystal will fill your home with a calm atmosphere, allowing divine energy to filter through, and helping you connect with angelic guides and your higher consciousness.

The soft energy emitted from celestite activates the throat, third eye and crown chakras, enabling you to develop your spiritual intuition easily. Lie in meditation, with pieces placed on these chakras, and you will find that you float into a deeper meditation effortlessly, picking up messages from spirit guides clearly. Fears and insecurities will disappear with this crystal in your home, as you realize you are safe and protected by your guides.

If a room in your home feels chaotic or full of emotional turbulence, place a piece of this light-blue crystal in a prominent place to create peaceful harmony. It brings back hope and optimism when you're grieving or sad, and encourages reconciliation, calm discussion and happier experiences in fraught relationships. Because of its ability to bring about tranquility, it's a perfect stone for the bedroom or meditation area, to enable you to smoothly drift into sleep or stillness of mind. It will help you with dream recall and even astral travel.

If you have children, place celestite in their bedrooms to help soothe any fears they may have, brought on by the darkness, and enable them to sleep more easily. This gem will also protect them with white light and bring their angel guides closer.

Placed in your workspace, celestite brings clarity of mind, focus and good fortune. Use this crystal here to help avoid stress and attract positive energies. It will stop you from feeling overwhelmed by a heavy workload, and help you feel restored after a long day. Artists, designers, musicians and anyone working in creative industries can benefit from celestite's inspirational boost. If you work giving readings or selling crystals, keep celestite with you all the time to maintain your spiritual connection, keep strong ethics and achieve prosperity.

The world's largest known geode, at over 30 feet wide, is made of celestite and was found on an island in Lake Erie. Discovered when making a well for a winery, the owner of the land has now converted it into a crystal cave for visitors.

Fluorite

BEST FOR:
Protection, organization, making progress.

LOOKS:
Comes in a variety of colors including green, blue, purple, clear and brown.

Fluorite is a highly protective crystal, both physically and on a psychic level. In the home it is highly effective at blocking harmful electromagnetic frequencies from computers and phones. This gem is a must to place on your desk and in your main living area. Create a protective fluorite grid around your computer, or place one between you and the tech that affects you in any way. In the right place, fluorite can combat effects of geopathic stress, coming from disrupted areas of the earth's magnetic field.

Meditate with it regularly and this gem will help you connect with your true self, enabling you to lose external influence. Fluorite stabilizes the aura, purifies negative energies, and clears stress, leaving you ready to go forward and make real progress.

It organizes everything from your body and mind to the clutter in your workspace and your relationships. In the living room, when free of external clutter, fluorite will encourage an uplifting atmosphere, making your gatherings go well and enhancing a sense of relaxation. Harmony and balance reign, especially if fluorite sits on a coffee table. People's negative opinions or other unwanted influences are deflected—it's a cloak around your aura.

Having fluorite in your home will bring structure to your daily life, help you learn and think quicker, as well as heighten spiritual and everyday awareness. If you work with a group, at work and especially in your home for healing circles, teaching sessions or meetings, yellow fluorite in the room will help bring unification. Encouraging a cooperative spirit, it may even make your family focus on a unified task that needs doing.

Green fluorite in particular works well in your yard, as it attracts butterflies. Meditate outside with it and you can tune into the nature spirits present. You can use this color of fluorite to heal damaged plants by charging it with that intention, holding it over the affected area and then placing it in the pot.

Blue fluorite in your home can calm or revitalize your energy, depending on what's needed. Try making an essence of it by leaving it in water overnight and spraying it into the room.

Energetically clear fluorite often, as it is such a protective crystal and soaks up a lot of negative energy. It likes to be placed in a stream or bowl of water overnight.

This crystal doesn't just work at home; you can keep its qualities working all day long by wearing fluorite earrings or holding and rubbing it as a palm stone.

Jet

BEST FOR:

Protection, absorbing negativity, grounding.

LOOKS:

Black like coal, but usually polished.

Jet is not a crystal but is, in fact, fossilized wood from antiquity. It's been found in graves for centuries. Used since the Bronze Age in jewelry and ornaments, the best was from northeast England, from where the Romans imported it to protect them from evil entities. From then on, it's been believed to protect from negative, draining energy, violence or illness.

Queen Victoria wore jet after the death of her husband, Prince Albert, as it was said to help with grief. If your home is full of sadness after trauma or the loss of a loved one, whether through death or divorce, place jet in the main living area. It helps you come to terms with a situation or relationship ending, so you can move on to the next phase of your life.

Jet will also alleviate anxiety and quash nightmares, so the children's bedrooms might need a jet crystal in them too. If your child has many worries, ask them to talk about them while holding the jet. Then bury the stone in your yard to take away their fears.

Place a piece of jet facing the front or back door to push bad vibes away. It will enable you to stay grounded and stabilize any area of your life, alleviate depression and help you let go of old emotions.

If you have money troubles, use jet to balance your finances and help you make headway in practically tackling your debts. Place it in your cash register at work, or in the wealth corner of your home—the far left back corner—to help turn your prosperity around.

If you're attracted to jet in a shop, you are likely to be an old soul, with many memories of past-life experiences. Meditate with it to help you access these, as jet acts as a gateway to the past and other dimensions for spiritual development. Jet links to the root chakra and awakens kundalini energy. Placed on your heart chakra when lying down in meditation, it will move that force up through all chakras to the crown, clearing your system inside and out.

If you've inherited jet jewelry that's been passed down for generations, make sure you cleanse it carefully before use, as it will have soaked up a lot of the previous wearers' energy. Bury jet in soil overnight to release it from the energy of others.

Jet is a purifier of all other stones. Simply place your crystals with jet in a bowl and leave them overnight.

Moss Agate

BEST FOR:

New beginnings, connecting with nature, calming animals.

LOOKS:

Milky white or translucent, with tendrils of manganese or iron that have made patterns like moss or lichen. Sometimes they can be dark green with blue inclusions.

With plant matter inside it, moss agate is often known as "the gardener's stone," as it encourages plant growth and agriculture. Many ancient cultures revered moss agate as a stone for good fortune, including Native Americans, who used it to bring rain. Europeans offered it to the spiritual guardians of the land in orchards, fields and gardens to get a good yield.

Plant this crystal with your plants, in a pot or flowerbed, to ensure that they stay healthy and abundant. Moss agate can help you communicate with nature spirits and devas who can assist with the success of your crops. A nurturing stone to encourage patience, peace and stability from the highs and lows of life, moss agate helps bring calm, especially when placed in your living area. It aids resilience, improves the positive parts of people's personalities, and helps everyone get along better. It is a wonderful crystal to place in the bedroom or meditation corner to help you quietly contemplate your spiritual growth and the interconnectedness of life.

According to feng shui, moss agate brings wood energy into your home, attracting good health, vitality and strength, especially for any new endeavors such as children or creative projects. Have one on the dinner table to boost nourishment from meals. Add one to your child's collection to ensure that they grow healthily. If you're starting a new project at work, place one on your desk to help it grow.

At work, moss agate in your office will slowly attract a promotion or raise. It especially boosts new businesses and is your talisman if you're self-employed. Keep a piece close by if doing your accounts or tax returns, and it will also help you save.

Moss agate helps pets, too. If they're overactive, nervous or aggressive, you can place a small stone under their bed to calm them down—this works especially well with animals from rescue centers. If you live in a city, moss agate in your cat's bed will restore their connection with nature. Moss agate can help the bond between children and pets, balancing both their energies in a positive way.

Depictions of the Virgin Mary, Jesus, John the Baptist, angels and various other human forms have manifested themselves in moss agate stones and can be found in churches and museums around the world.

Shungite

BEST FOR:
Grounding, healing and protecting from radiation and electromagnetic smog.

LOOKS:
Black, oily or dull-looking; or elite shungite, which has a silvery tint to it and sometimes gold inclusions.

Although shungite has been on the planet for at least two million years, its use in homes around the world is relatively recent. Its carbon mineral makeup contains fullerenes, which conduct electricity yet shield from electromagnetic frequency and radiation from modern technology. Fullerenes contain powerful antioxidants that absorb and eliminate harm in our environment and from our bodies. Research on fullerenes won three scientists the Nobel Prize in chemistry in 1996.

Historically, water infused with shungite was drunk to promote healing. Russian czar Peter the Great is said to have visited the region where shungite was discovered, and used the power-packed water for its beneficial properties.

Soak a chunk of the duller shungite in a bottle of water overnight to purify the water and fill it with the mineral's healing antioxidants to boost your immune system and general well-being. Drinking this two or three times a day will help detoxify the body of any pollutants and maintain healthy cell growth. Testing has also revealed shungite to be able to absorb pesticides, free radicals and bacteria from the body. It can even prevent and lessen the symptoms of colds.

Shungite is a must for your home; reduce electromagnetic radiation by placing stones or pyramids of it at the base of devices such as your cell phone, laptop or wifi router. You can even get shungite discs to stick on the back of your phone to soak up the potentially damaging EMF rays. Carry one with you if you're traveling through airports, to protect you from the energy emitted by security scanners.

Shungite activates all the chakras, boosting energy and clearing the mind of all negativity. If your emotions are up and down, or you worry a lot, meditating with shungite in your hand allows light to fill your body and your aura, keeping anxiety, depression and external negative energy at bay.

If you suffer from insomnia or tension headaches, try placing a shungite sphere or pyramid by your bed to combat the effects of stress. It's a good grounding stone, so it's worth placing in your yard, and sitting or lying on the ground and meditating while holding it, to give your body a stronger, healing connection to the earth.

You can now get shungite paint for the walls of your house to protect against electromagnetic frequency coming from outside sources, such as smart meters, solar panels and street lights.

Smoky Quartz

BEST FOR:

Grounding, protecting, dispelling negative energy.

LOOKS:

Translucent quartz turning gray, smoky, yellowish, brown or black.

Originally called morion when it was discovered and used by the Druids and Celts around 300BCE, smoky quartz is the national gem of Scotland. Here it became common in Highlander adornment, and is one of the power stones on the handle of the Scottish dagger, which is still part of the country's national costume.

Smoky quartz is exceptional at clearing negative energies, grounding your physical body, and eliminating stress. Place one in your bedroom if you have trouble sleeping to stop your mind from racing and help you drift off into a deep slumber.

It's another good stone to use to block geopathic and electromagnetic waves that can harm the body. Place it by your cordless phone or above disturbed ley lines to stop their energy from affecting you. Or sit holding this crystal when you feel overloaded by "electrosmog."

Linking with the root chakra, this powerful crystal will increase your connection to the earth, inspiring environmental concern and pride at being incarnated in human form at this time. It brings strength and stability as well as protection from psychic attack or emotional and physical stress. Stand in your yard, on the grass, with your smoky quartz in your receptive hand pointing downwards, and feel any negativity drain out of you and into the earth.

This crystal also protects your home, workplace or vehicle from theft or damage by others. Add a small stone to your wallet, bag or glove compartment of your car to ensure safety. In your car, smoky quartz is also thought to protect against road rage, mechanical breakdowns and other driving dangers.

Use smoky quartz in all the main areas of your house to counter bad moods or nasty comments that bring you down. Let its energy lift depression, promote positive thoughts and bring passion and vitality into your life.

If bullying or gossip occurs in the workplace, lay dark smoky quartz pointing outwards on your desk in a semi-circle to help you stay calm and concentrate on getting the job done. Wear it as a pendant to boost your survival instincts and help your career goals manifest. If you need to stay rational, get organized or focus on any calculations, place this crystal near you to help. You may see more psychic phenomena such as ghosts, spirit guides or UFOs when wearing or carrying smoky quartz, as it draws these into your auric field to make them easier for you to perceive.

Turquoise

BEST FOR:

Leadership qualities, clear communication, prosperity and success.

LOOKS:

Turquoise copper aluminum material, with greenish speckles of iron.

Turquoise is one of the oldest stones used by humans, with beads dating back to 5000BCE found in Iran. In Ancient Egypt, where it was mined in 3200BCE, Hathor, the goddess of love, marriage, music and women, was known as the Lady of Turquoise. In many Native American cultures, it was seen as a male power stone that only warriors were allowed to wear. In Mexican ruins, 9,000 turquoise beads were found in a single warrior chief's grave.

At home, turquoise brings both male and female energies into balance, enhancing communication between the sexes, bringing empathy, creativity and inner calm along with strength, ambition and alertness. It stimulates romantic love and works to create a restorative atmosphere encouraging well-being, success and good luck. Rest while holding turquoise if you're feeling exhausted, panicky or down in any way, and let it lift your low mood. A purification stone,

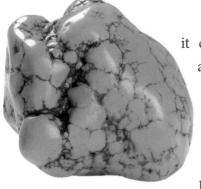

it clears negativity from the mind, and also electromagnetic smog from your external surroundings.

Turquoise is sometimes called "the campaigner's stone" because it will bring strength and leadership to those protecting the environment or taking peaceful action to protect human rights. Wearing it as a necklace will help calm your nerves if you have to speak in public. Working on balancing the throat chakra, it helps you express yourself effectively and clearly communicate any repressed feelings that may be holding you back from your true potential.

At work, keep turquoise with financial documents or accounts to attract wealth by making shrewd investments. Wearing it can lead to promotion or increased travel for work—and it will also protect your possessions from theft. It's a useful crystal for many professions: accountants, and anyone using computers, can use turquoise to help relax their minds; it helps cure writer's block and ease performance anxiety in anyone working in television or radio; and laborers should carry it to protect them from physical injury.

Traditionally, turquoise was braided into a horse's mane to stop it from stumbling. At home, if you place a piece of turquoise near stairs, it can prevent falling, especially in children or the elderly. Children can carry this stone to combat shyness and stop bullying. A pet with a piece of turquoise attached to its collar will not get lost or stolen. Turquoise should ideally be given as a gift, not bought for oneself.

Household problem = crystal solution

For most household problems, there's a crystal that can help.

MESSY, CHAOTIC HOUSE

Fluorite organizes inside and out to bring harmony and structure to you daily life and help clear your clutter.

PEOPLE ARGUING AND NOT GETTING ALONG

Blue lace agate on your coffee table or dining table should ease conversations and stop anyone from saying anything they might regret. Place a large piece of amber in your living space to guard against conflict, transform negative vibes into positive, and dispel any sadness or anxiety.

NOISY NEIGHBORS

Put rose quartz next to the wall between you and your angry neighbors to calm their shouting and promote peace.

HYPERACTIVE CHILDREN OR PETS

Purple fluorite helps dogs behave better when they're outdoors, and helps children calm down, while moss agate balances both when placed in their beds.

UNHELPFUL TEENAGERS

Place amazonite in their bedroom to help them get out of bed at a reasonable time and live a healthier lifestyle.

Ametrine will do the same, and will keep teens out of trouble.

ALLEVIATING NIGHTMARES

A piece of jet in the room or held in the hand to soothe someone before bed works wonders to quash bad dreams.

PLANTS KEEP DYING

If your plants are affected by central heating and look like they're wilting, place moss agate crystals in the soil.

Fluorite can mend damaged plants; simply pass it over the affected area, then bury the stone in the pot.

TECHNOLOGY MAKING YOU LETHARGIC AND SICK

If you're affected by electromagnetic frequency, wear shungite or stick a disc of it to the back of your cell phone.

You can also create a special grid of protection with shungite, black tourmaline or smoky quartz by placing small pieces of it in the corner of each room in your home to transform negative energies. Try joining the crystals in your mind, or using a quartz wand to protect your entire home.

Key crystals for each area

AT THE FRONT DOOR

- ✧ This is a key place to put crystals to keep away any unwanted visitors and attract good vibes only. To protect the whole home from harmful energies, place smoky quartz, black tourmaline or jet in the doorway.
- ✧ To attract only good vibes, place carnelian just inside the front door; if it's abundance you're after, use citrine.

LIVING ROOM

- ✧ A large piece of rose quartz or jade in your living space will bring love and harmony throughout the whole home.
- ✧ Place a wand of selenite on the coffee table to fill the place with positive light.
- ✧ Tiger's eye placed in a prominent position will help bring harmony to any turbulent family relationships.
- ✧ Labradorite will inject some fun into your home if you've been stuck in a rut.

DINING ROOM

✧ Amber or carnelian on the dining table will help stimulate healthy appetites.

✧ Citrine in the center of the room is said to keep conversation positive while you eat, as well as assisting with digestion.

✧ Orange calcite will create lively debate while keeping it upbeat and respectful.

KITCHEN

✧ To stimulate creative, confident cooking with ease, choose carnelian for kitchen surfaces.

✧ Red jasper is also energizing, and will wake you up in the morning as you make breakfast.

BEDROOM

FOR DEEP SLEEP

✧ Either sleep with a small smooth stone of amethyst or moonstone under your pillow or bed, or place a piece of rose quartz on your bedside table. Alternatively, soak an amethyst in water overnight and drink it before bedtime.

BETTER LOVE LIFE

✧ Turquoise balances the sexes and stimulates romantic love. If you want to bring creativity and calm, along with strength and alertness into the bedroom, place a piece of turquoise on both sides of the bed.

OFFICE

TO COMBAT STRESS

✧ A black obsidian sphere or a dish of smaller tumbled stones will rebalance your workload.

FOR CREATIVITY

✧ Place clear quartz on your desk to ignite creativity, but balance it with lapis lazuli so you don't work too late into the night.

FOR CREATIVITY AND GOOD FORTUNE

✧ Celestite on your desk will get your creative juices flowing and ease stress.

FOR WEALTH AND ABUNDANCE

✧ Citrine in your wallet, on your financial documents, and in the career area (far left corner from the door) will attract success. Turquoise will also have this effect.

BATHROOM

✧ Have a dish of your favorite crystals here to add to bathwater for a boost. Jade will restore your tired body, rose quartz soothes frayed nerves, clear quartz added to your bath will energize, and turquoise will bring inspired ideas while you soak.

GARDEN

✧ Green aventurine helps plant roots fill with energy, and boosts plant growth, as does moss agate planted with your crops.

✧ Charge a clear quartz with your intention to grow a beautiful garden, or a reminder to water your plants regularly, and place the crystal in your outside space to work its magic.

Which crystal for which zodiac sign?

Each zodiac sign has a few crystals that work best with it, because they either emanate a similar energy, or give your astrological personality a boost. Choose gifts for yourself, family and friends from the appropriate gems to boost your astrological traits as you wear them as jewelry or place them in prominent positions in your home to let their planetary influence fill your rooms.

ARIES

March 21—April 20

Diamond, bloodstone, pyrite, hematite, jasper

GEMINI

May 22—June 21

Citrine, white sapphire, ametrine, green aventurine

TAURUS

April 21—May 21

Rose quartz, emerald, peridot

CANCER

June 22—July 22

Moonstone, pearl, selenite, sodalite

LEO

July 23—August 23

Carnelian, topaz, tiger's eye, amber, clear quartz

SAGITTARIUS

November 23—December 21

Turquoise, ruby, azurite, rhodochrosite, iolite

VIRGO

August 24—September 22

Moss agate, blue sapphire, amazonite, yellow aragonite

CAPRICORN

December 22—January 20

Black onyx, garnet, jet, smoky quartz

LIBRA

September 23—October 23

Opal, lapis lazuli, celestite, rose quartz

AQUARIUS

January 21—February 18

Amethyst, sugilite, blue lace agate, angelite, moldavite

SCORPIO

24 October—November 22

Black obsidian, apache tear, coral, labradorite, malachite

PISCES

February 19—March 20

Jade, aquamarine, purple fluorite, kyanite

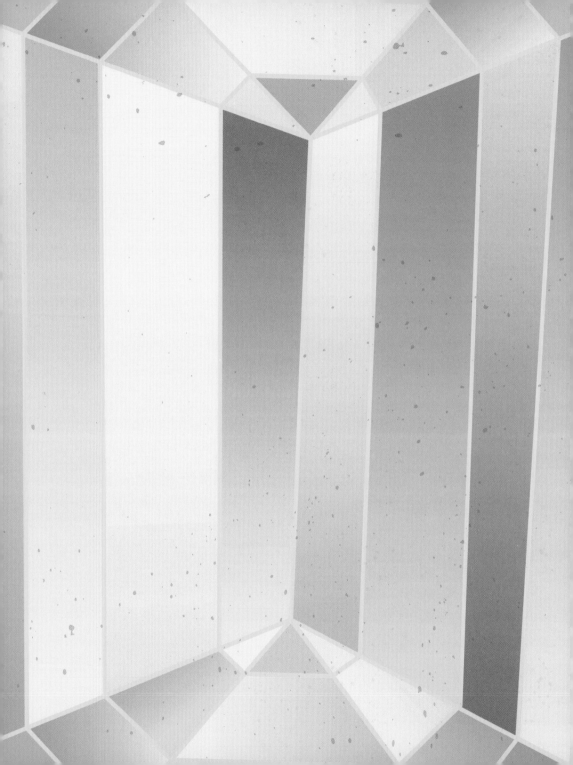

The Crystals That Are Best For Healing

Connect with certain crystals often to create a nourishing, holistic healing practice for yourself and to help you heal others, including your pets and the planet.

Healing with crystals

For centuries, crystals have been used for healing by expert practitioners and ordinary men and women wanting a gentle yet effective way to boost health and well-being. The right gems used in the right way can alleviate physical symptoms such as headaches, itchy skin and an upset stomach, and deeper emotional wounds, including post-traumatic stress or heartbreak, and mental anguish holding you back. They can give you a general energy increase, protect you from harmful electromagnetic frequency from electronic devices and ease the effects of arthritis, menopause or diabetes. Once you've figured out which crystals work best with your energy or ailment, there are various ways you can use them to holistically heal yourself and others.

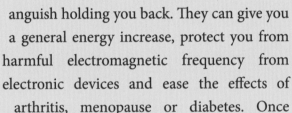

The following ten crystals are some of the main ones for healing specific things. If you're just starting out, you can also use amethyst, citrine, rose quartz or clear quartz as powerful general healers of auras, emotions and atmosphere.

HOW CRYSTALS HEAL

Crystals emit a certain energy according to what they're made of, their color, and what they've been programmed to do by your focused attention. They work by vibrating a frequency that influences the mind, body and spirit, through your senses, your aura and your home.

Some crystals contain minerals widely known to help balance the body. Malachite, for example, contains copper, which is used to reduce inflammation and prevent swelling. These can be worn on the body, or carried in a pouch or in your pocket. Some can even be drunk as a specially made elixir (except for malachite, which can be toxic).

MAKING A CRYSTAL ELIXIR

Many crystals can be made into an elixir to boost health simply by placing a piece of the gem in a glass bottle of distilled or pure mineral water overnight. This can then be drunk to get the crystal benefits into the body, or heated and used as a topical solution for skin problems that the crystal might help with.

CLEARING AND ACTIVATING THE CHAKRAS

Other stones work on cleansing or stimulating the chakras when placed above their location on the body. This keeps the energy within you and your aura sparkling and working well. It also activates the areas of your psyche connected to them. For example, self-love is connected to the heart chakra, and confidence is linked to the solar plexus.

See page 35 for which crystals to use for which chakras. Then place the correct ones down the center of the body—yours or whoever you are giving a healing to—while lying down in meditation.

Relax for 20-30 minutes to let the crystals' energy take effect on the chakras beneath them, cleansing, balancing and energizing your whole system.

DIFFERENT WAYS TO HEAL

Other ways to absorb crystal energy include sleeping with a specific stone under your pillow or creating a healing grid of the crystals in the room where you want it to have an effect. You can also add crystals to your bathwater, to soak in their power.

Use your intuition and discernment to guide you in choosing the right crystal and where to place it. If there's a specific physical ailment you or someone else wants help with, simply place a small stone on the area, or hold it close to it for as long as you can, imagining its healing energy working its way to the problem.

HEALING YOURSELF

Before you start any healing, you may want to ask for support and protection from divine sources, such as the angels, a healing god or goddess, or your higher consciousness to work through you for the highest good. Hold your crystal in your hands and place it to your heart, filling it with love and asking that it do what's best for you or your patient.

Through meditation, by holding the healing crystal in your hands, you can absorb its powerful energy. Sit quietly and take some deep breaths. When you exhale, let out all negative thoughts and feelings.

As you breathe in, imagine the crystal's positive light filling your whole body. Visualize this energy as a soothing, warm liquid radiating from your heart to fill you up, expanding out into your aura as well. Sit peacefully feeling your crystal's energy making you whole and happy.

Once a week, you could try sitting inside a circle of different colored crystals laid out on the floor. See each of the rainbow of colors coming into your aura and being absorbed by your body for a full top-up of their energy. Red crystals will energize you, green will nurture you, and orange boosts creativity. Pink will fill you with love, blue helps clear communication, and purple links to higher realms. Afterwards, make sure you ground yourself and ask for protection from a black crystal such as jet or obsidian.

Alternatively, lie down comfortably and position the different colored crystals on top of their corresponding chakras for a complete cleansing of your whole mind, body and spirit as you rest.

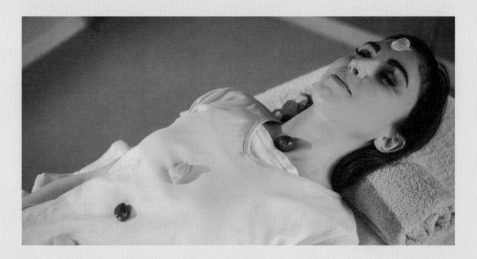

HEALING OTHERS

Contact healing is when the person being healed is present at the session. It doesn't mean you make contact with the crystal and their body. Usually the gem is held a couple of inches above the patient's body, always fully clothed. Listen to your intuition and sense the energy of the crystal regarding where it wants to be positioned and for how long. You may want to hold it in a certain area or move it gently and continuously over your patient.

When completed, always say a few words of thanks to your higher power and the crystal for its work. Remember to cleanse it well after every healing session if it absorbs energy.

DISTANT HEALING

You can also use crystals to send healing energy to people, groups or animals, as well as the oceans, earth or specific areas of the world that need help. Choose green or brown crystals, such as moss agate or jade, to heal the land or forests and the creatures that dwell there. Blue gems, including aquamarine or blue coral, work wonders on the waters of the world and the fish that swim in them. Tiger's eye or leopardskin jasper help endangered species stay healthy and strong.

Hold a larger crystal in your hands. Focus on filling the stone with prayers and intentions to heal whatever you've chosen to help. Say your wish out loud repeatedly into the crystal, or chant a healing mantra for it to absorb.

Inhale deeply and imagine the light from the crystal filling you up. Exhale any darkness. Continue to breathe in light until you are full of sparkling positive healing energy. Then send this healing light to your chosen subject as you breathe out, still saying the healing prayer or mantra in your mind. Visualize the healing taking place, and the person, pet or area shining with health and vitality.

You could also place the charged crystal on a photo of the absent friend, animal or place to be healed, and leave it there for as long as you want it to work its magic.

Amazonite

BEST FOR:
Soothing and communicating emotions rationally, encouraging a healthy lifestyle, blocking microwaves.

LOOKS:
Blue-green or turquoise opaque, sometimes darker green with white lines.

Amazonite has been used for healing and good fortune for centuries. It is believed to have featured on the breastplates of warrior women in the matriarchal Bronze Age tribe of Amazonians. Easy to carve, amazonite was made into beads and other jewelry by the early Mesopotamians, and into a scarab ring in King Tutankhamen's tomb. Found growing in slabs, the ancient Egyptian *Book of the Dead* was carved into it.

A crystal of courage and truth, it helps you bravely communicate what is true for you, and know and state your boundaries clearly. Often called the "peacemaker" stone, it enables you to see another viewpoint and, when placed in a room, will emanate peaceful vibes for reconciliation and healing. It can help you rectify inner conflicts.

Amazonite connects to and rebalances the heart and throat chakras, soothing turbulent emotions and assisting with honest, heartfelt communication. If you need to have a difficult conversation, put some amazonite in your pocket and let it help your words flow with compassion and kindness.

When self-healing with crystals, place a piece of amazonite on your throat to fully awaken this chakra and help this area of your body function better. Drink its essence in water to boost calcium intake and ease muscle spasms. Amazonite calms the nervous system, supports the thyroid gland, and encourages both men and women to live a healthy lifestyle.

Used often, amazonite will bring the masculine and feminine sides of your personality into balance—and in the workplace it is thought to combat sexism. It also harmonizes your intuition with your intellect, helping you feel what you need to do in the world and then bravely go and do it. If you have something you'd like to manifest, state it clearly to your amazonite and meditate with it often to activate your intention.

Amazonite is a powerful crystal to block electromagnetic emanations from your cell phone or computer; stick some to your phone or position it between you and the devices you use. Placed on your desk, it will bring focus to your purpose and success in your endeavors. In the kitchen, it will block microwave harm from gadgets as well as encourage other family members to help with household jobs.

Cleanse amazonite with a mint infusion to recharge its considerable powers.

Aquamarine

BEST FOR:
Water healing, increased intuition, clearing the throat chakra.

LOOKS:
Very light blue, clear to opaque.

This crystal-clear blue type of beryl was believed to be mermaids' treasure in ancient times. It was called "water of the sea" by Roman fishermen, who carried it with them for courage and safety on the oceans. It was also used by physicians to aid digestion and decrease fluid retention. Roman craftsmen made goblets from it to purify water.

Still believed to be purifying, you can make an aquamarine detox elixir to cleanse the body. Soak a stone in water overnight and drink it to soothe stomach pains, boost the immune and lymphatic systems, and clear the throat of infections or soreness. Soothing for tired or irritated eyes, it is even believed to help vision. Place a small, smooth tumbled stone on the eyelids for 20 minutes each night while you relax and let its cooling, calming properties take effect.

Aquamarine is one of the most powerful crystals for activating and clearing the throat chakra, helping you express yourself honestly with an open heart and greater confidence. Having it in your home will harmonize the atmosphere and keep angry emotions at bay, as well as assist in clearing out clutter mentally, emotionally and physically.

Meditating with it will bring acceptance of your true self, a deeper wisdom, and enable you to let go of built-up emotions. It's a lovely stone to receive courage and healing from if you're suffering from grief or going through major changes.

A powerful stone to boost psychic and spiritual development, use aquamarine to send absent healing to others. Place it on a photo of the person you want to help and imagine aquamarine's healing energy filling their body, aligning their chakras and bringing them back to full health.

You can also charge it with prayers to clean the oceans and protect all sea creatures, as it is especially linked with whales and dolphins. Place a piece of aquamarine on a picture of any endangered ocean life while seeing them thriving for decades to come. Feel the sparkling health of the waters of the world in your heart and let that energy ripple out around the planet. Closer to home, add some to your fish tank or pond to keep the marine creatures healthy.

With its gentle, compassionate energy, aquamarine encourages compromise, negotiation and service. It helps you take responsibility for yourself and others less fortunate, and assists humanity to become more healing, bringing natural justice and balance to our destructive and damaging habits.

Cleanse aquamarine in a blue glass bowl of seawater or salted mineral water on the night of a full moon, rinsing with pure water afterwards.

Aragon Star Clusters

BEST FOR:
Earth healing, grounding, stress relief.

LOOKS:
Mainly orange, gold and brown "sputnik" clusters, but also found in white, yellow, green and blue.

Aragonite is mostly found in spiky cluster formations of tube-shaped crystals exploding from a central point. Named after the Aragon River in Spain, where it was discovered in 1790, aragonite is a great grounding stone to bring you back into balance after stressful episodes. Balancing the heart and mind, it will help you stop focusing negatively on difficult situations and bring renewed strength and faith in your ability to meet any challenge.

A stone to encourage new beginnings, aragonite brings

stability, discipline and a pragmatic way of doing things, as well as a clearer mind and motivation. With aragonite in your home, family members might get better at timekeeping and tackle those chores today rather than next week!

Meditating with an aragonite cluster regularly will help you nourish yourself physically (by eating healthy regular meals) and emotionally (by taking time out to calm frayed nerves). It's a good gem to use to prepare for meditation because it raises your vibrations to a higher level spiritually and gives the body a boost of vitality.

Healers benefit from starting any session of healing by tuning into aragonite's energy to center themselves before working on others. Have aragonite around if you're going to do any smudging or dowsing to link strongly into the Earth Goddess energy to support you.

This crystal activates the root chakra and the earth chakra below our feet, deeply connecting us to mother earth. Feeling the ground beneath you while standing holding an aragonite star cluster will help you discern what healing the planet needs, and how to get it to it. If you suddenly feel an urge to ditch plastic, or plant trees everywhere you go, that's the effect of aragonite in your life.

With strong powers to heal the planet, it's no surprise that aragonite can clear geopathic stress or blocked ley lines. To do this, either place the stone on a map over the area you wish to send healing energy to, or, if you're able to visit, perform a healing ceremony, cleansing the crystal, programming it with prayers, and then planting it the soil.

To cleanse, bury aragonite in a pot of soil for a full day and night.

Blue Kyanite

BEST FOR:
Connecting with and healing the animal kingdom, attuning to the spirit world, increasing telepathy.

LOOKS:
Shards or blades of blue-white, opaque with a pearly sheen or transparent.

Blue kyanite is a fairly new crystal for healing and other spiritual work, found abundantly in Brazil. It's a powerful stone for connecting and attuning with animals of all kinds, plants and humans. It quickly calms the mind and body, allowing you to go deep into meditation, attuning swiftly with spirit guides, psychic powers and your own intuition.

This blue crystal stimulates the third eye and throat chakras, boosting your communication skills and self-expression while linking that with your deepest truth and higher guidance. It's also a great gem for aligning all chakras to clear your body's pathways for better healing, and attunement to the spiritual realm for help.

Use blue kyanite when performing healing to create a stronger link between you and the person or creature being healed. Work with it to send or receive healing energy and boost telepathy with friends, family

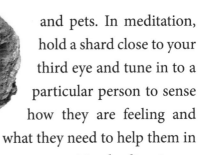

and pets. In meditation, hold a shard close to your third eye and tune in to a particular person to sense how they are feeling and what they need to help them in any way, or conjure up a positive healing image in your mind and send it to them. It can also assist you in astral travel or lucid dreaming—place it on your third eye when lying down before going to sleep.

Blades of blue kyanite make excellent wands to brush away any negative energy from others, dispelling anger, frustration and illusion. They make a soothing gift for anyone passing away to help them ground spiritual energy into their body so they can transition into the spirit world more smoothly.

Make a healing grid of blue kyanite to help you stop any self-destructive behavior patterns or if you feel you've moved away from your true path. Place rows of small kyanite shards coming out in six different directions from a central kyanite stone and meditate with this layout every night until you regain clarity. Lowering your gaze to just focus on the crystals, allow your mind to wander, allowing images and ideas to take form as they arise, bringing you insight, guidance and aligning you to your highest frequency again.

Kyanite does not absorb negative energy, so it never needs to be cleansed, but you can rejuvenate it by leaving it near plants first thing in the morning.

Carnelian

BEST FOR:

Healing from abuse, trusting yourself, and rejuvenating your relationships.

LOOKS:

Bright orange to red, semi-translucent glassy pebble, often containing lighter or darker spots and streaks.

The Latin root for this crystal's name means "flesh," and carnelian can certainly give your body a boost. Expect better health and vitality, plus increased metabolism and sex drive, when working with this vibrant orange or red stone of confidence and courage. Ancient warriors wore it around their necks to make them bold in battle, and it has long been believed to bring shy people out of their shells.

Carnelian is a very healing stone: it gives you energy, passion and motivation, as well as bringing abundance in all areas of your life. It is also believed to help the body heal after injury, whether physical or emotional, and it's well known for healing

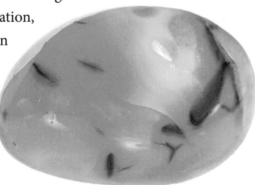

after abuse. It enables you to trust yourself and your perceptions again so that you can take the lead in your own joyful and fulfilling life.

As well as increasing creativity and concentration, it also rejuvenates relationships. Place a piece of carnelian under the corners of your mattress to bring passion and stamina back to the bedroom. Stimulating the lower three chakras, but especially the root chakra, it will boost libido and fertility, alleviate sexual anxieties, and ease menstrual or menopausal symptoms. Place a piece of carnelian on the skin at the solar plexus while lying down in meditation, and allow its surge of energy to work from that chakra down, balancing and grounding you as well.

Carnelian connects you more to your inner self while anchoring you in present reality. This, in turn, supports you to detox and heal from addiction to substances, especially any related to low self-esteem. Working with this gem will bring acceptance of life as well as less fear of death. It is beneficial for the elderly to carry carnelian in their pockets to lift the mood, and for men going through a mid-life crisis.

Honour this crystal's love of community spirit to gather with like-minded friends to use carnelian to send healing to ancient sacred sites or derelict buildings to preserve them. Ask a carnelian stone to heal the environment around it, then bury it in the earth. Or make an essence of carnelian with water and pour this onto the affected area.

If you have a bowl of gems in your home, add carnelian to it, as it cleanses other crystals.

Hematite

BEST FOR:
Grounding and balancing, cleansing the blood, healing the spine.

LOOKS:
Metallic gray heavy iron oxide, sometimes found in brown-red shades. Forms in rough rosettes but more often found smoothed shiny.

Hematite is iron oxide found commonly in iron ore all over the world. It also forms in quartz. Although mostly a metallic gray, some hematite has reddish brown streaks and marks in red when rough-cut and rubbed against another stone. Its name comes from the Greek word for blood, due to its color when ground into a powder.

So it's no surprise that hematite helps heal your blood, by cleansing it, stimulating iron absorption and boosting circulation, even easing heavy menstruation and bringing down blood pressure. Believed to regenerate tissue and help make red blood cells, it can also draw heat out of your body and be drunk as an elixir or placed on the forehead to soothe fevers.

An incredible stone for self-healing, hematite can actually pull out pain. Lie comfortably and hold a piece of hematite over the pain or the solar plexus chakra, and allow it to draw the ill feeling away.

Hematite has a strong grounding ability, pulling the root chakra down to the earth to align and balance you, making it useful for balancing emotions and aligning your spine.

Ask a friend to help with this healing: lie down on your front and have them place a piece of hematite at the top of your spine, one at the bottom and one on the problematic area. Relax with your head to one side and visualize your back fully healed. This eases the way for realignment and grounds your energy through your spine. Just don't lie like this for very long or if inflammation is present.

With its high iron content, hematite has a magnetic pull, which can attract the right opportunities to turn your dreams into reality. If worked with regularly, it can restore harmony to the body, focus the mind on figuring out practical problems, and enhance willpower and tenacity. Hematite is also known as the lawyer's stone, because it helps justice prevail in legal wrangles or neighborly disputes.

Spiritually, it was used for divination and polished into mirrors to deflect negativity in ancient times. Hematite is one to have on your meditation altar to stop negative energies entering your aura, especially during astral travel, which it stimulates.

Carry hematite with you during and after flying, as its power is said to combat jet lag.

Malachite

BEST FOR:
Purifying, protection and transforming negative energies to positive.

LOOKS:
Rich, vibrant green with swirling and eye-shaped darker or lighter green bands.

Raw malachite can be toxic, and should never be used by children or with animals, but in its more common, polished form it has been used for healing for centuries. Mined as long ago as 4000BCE, malachite was used in Ancient Egypt as a power stone to channel higher energy to earth. To help pharaohs be wiser leaders, they lined their headdresses with it. Malachite was also ground into a powder eyeshadow believed to enhance vision and spiritual insight.

A powerful protection stone since the Middle Ages, when it was thought to shield people from the "evil eye," malachite absorbs negative energy and pollutants from the environment and the body. It soaks up radiation and plutonium damage, and clears electromagnetic pollution when placed near televisions, computers, microwaves and other technology that emits harmful rays. Place at least two crystals in each room with any gadgets or fluorescent lighting in to combat toxic effects. Carry a small, smooth stone with you when on a plane to counteract radiation from flying.

Malachite draws out impurities, pain and inflammation from the body if placed carefully over the affected area, with a small cloth underneath. Lie down with a piece on your abdomen to relieve menstrual cramps or a stomach ache, or place on the jaw to ease a toothache. This healing gem is also believed to boost the immune system and circulation, stimulate cell regeneration and liver function and lower blood pressure. Worn around the waist, it is believed to help keep diabetes at bay (but it should never replace the advice of your doctor!). Many believe that malachite is still evolving, and will become one of the most important healing stones of the future.

A stone of transformation, it encourages deep emotional healing when placed on the solar plexus during a lying-down meditation. Allow it to bring suppressed feelings and past traumas up to be released, and show you what is stopping your spiritual growth. Then place it on the heart chakra to open you up to unconditional love. Add a gentler crystal to this process, such as rose quartz or rhodonite, as using malachite can mean intense mood swings and sudden change. If it causes heart palpitations, replace it with either of these stones to calm.

Because malachite absorbs so much, it needs to be cleansed regularly under running water. This gradually weakens the stone; when it eventually crumbles, bury it in soil, as its work is complete.

Moonstone

BEST FOR:
Boosting fertility of plants and women, easing menstrual or menopause symptoms, calming emotions.

LOOKS:
Translucent white, dusky pink, gray, yellow and sometimes blue, all displaying a pearly opalescence.

Looking like the moon shimmering in the night sky, this crystal carries the intuitive and feminine powers of our lunar guide and links us to nature's cycles. This boosts fertility and helps with menstruation and menopause issues, including easing PMS, fluid retention and hot flashes. For men, it helps them tune into their more feminine side, balancing aggressiveness.

Moonstone is said to lose its silvery sheen if the person using it holds too much anger inside them. It also changes color and should be used for different purposes according to the lunation. As the moon waxes to its fullest, moonstone will grow deeper in color, yet more translucent, and should be used for healing and manifestation. As the moon wanes, the gem will grow paler and emit more gentle energy conducive to rest and reflection on your inner world, calming emotions and soothing nerves.

Outside, use moonstone to help your garden grow well. Plant herbs or salad greens three days before the full moon—traditionally the peak growth time for plants—and bury a piece of moonstone with them to increase yield. Growing your garden according to biodynamic forces, using the lunar cycle, shows there is a right time to plant and the right time to harvest—in the garden and in life.

Moonstone has long been associated with love, especially in India, where it is given as a wedding gift to encourage harmony and fidelity between lovers. Made into jewelry in ancient Rome and Eastern European cultures, wearing moonstone is said to attract a new lover. Women meditating with it regularly will stimulate their kundalini energy and sex drive, and it's the biggest crystal booster of fertility.

Wearing a moonstone necklace when you make love at the time of the full moon should synchronize your body with the lunar cycle, helping you figure out your most fertile time to conceive. Or you could try making a fertility grid in the bedroom, with 12 moonstones in a circle around the bed and a 13th stone centrally positioned underneath. Moonstone in the bedroom generally encourages sleep and banishes anxiety and nightmares, especially for children.

For healing others, hold some moonstone close to your heart, filling it with loving energy, and then giving it to someone who is going through a tough time emotionally.

Orange Calcite

BEST FOR:
Boosting self-esteem and vitality, expressing sexuality and healing sexual wounds.

LOOKS:
Soft, warm light orange, waxy looking, sometimes banded.

Sunshine-colored orange calcite lifts the mood like no other crystal, dissolving problems, fears and depression. Legend says that orange calcite was thrown from the Baltic sun goddess Saule's chariot as she drove across the sky to begin the long journey to overcome the darkness at Winter Solstice on December 21st.

A balancing stone, it will increase confidence and self-esteem as well as motivate you to be more energetic in all areas of your life. Placed prominently in the home, orange calcite will clear it of negative or stagnant energy, and give everyone who lives there a boost of endorphins and positivity.

If your creativity or sexuality has felt blocked, orange calcite is the crystal to help heal this aspect of your life. Positioned on any of the lower three chakras when lying down in meditation, it will cleanse all three and energize your whole system, reigniting inspiration, enthusiasm and passion. Working with orange calcite is especially gentle but effective if there has been dysfunction, fear or trauma that has created psychological scars around your sexuality.

Meditate lying down with a piece of orange calcite above your groin area and visualize its vitality boosting your sexual energy and circulating around your whole body to radiate out into the world. It will help you and others embrace your sexuality, however it may present itself.

Women trying to conceive should carry orange calcite with them to balance their hormones and increase fertility. You may even want to create a fertility grid around your bed with a circle of orange calcite crystals surrounding it. This will also promote calm, restful sleep and turn stress into serenity, relaxing mind and body fully.

Placed on the abdomen, orange calcite can help heal the reproductive system and intestines, soothe kidneys and bladder issues, and alleviate symptoms of Irritable Bowel Syndrome. Make an elixir of calcite to drink to increase calcium absorption, boost the immune system, and stimulate healthy tissue growth. This can also be applied to the skin to treat warts, ulcers and wounds.

Recharge calcite as well as yourself by adding it to your bath and soaking by candlelight. When it crumbles, its work is done, so bury it in soil with gratitude for all of its healing help.

Rhodochrosite

BEST FOR:
Healing sexual abuse and emotional wounds, attracting new love or renewing passion, healing Mother Earth.

LOOKS:
Vivid raspberry pink, rose-red and orange, with swirls and circular patterned banding. Usually polished smooth.

Also known as "Rosa del Inca," rhodochrosite is only occasionally found in silver mines, where the Incan ruler Viracocha discovered it in the 12th or 13th century, in northern Argentina. According to the indigenous people of the Andes, the stunning pinkish-red stone was made from the blood of their royal ancestors, and was believed to be a stone of strength, stamina and powerful love.

Rhodochrosite's energy of love is more dynamic and intense than rose quartz. It encourages greater self-love and compassion, and will guide you toward happiness in love after pain or doubt. It is very effective at healing emotional wounds, post-traumatic stress and other issues after sexual abuse. Often known as the "inner child stone," it brings loving awareness to the truth of any childhood experiences. It helps you understand and forgive your parents or anyone else for mistakes, releasing the past so you can love confidently again.

When placed over the heart chakra in meditation, let rhodochrosite's peaceful energy fill your aura, heal your past and show you that you are deeply loved just as you are. By meditating often with this crystal, you will experience the blissful energy of universal love. This can also help with overcoming addictions that stem from having low self-esteem.

Use rhodochrosite to send loving, healing energy to mother earth. Tune in to the gem's power and ask: "How may I best serve the world?" Let your joyful ideas and inspired urges lead the way.

This healing stone contains manganese, which helps the body repair itself. Taken in an elixir, it can relieve ear or sinus infections, inflammations such as stomach ulcers, and other abdominal pain. If you suffer from migraines, try placing a piece of rhodochrosite at the base of the skull.

It is also soothing for skin disorders, including hives, rashes or shingles. Make a topical solution by placing a piece of rhodochrosite in distilled or spring water in sunlight for a few days to energize it. Heat the water gently and soak a cloth it in to dab on the affected area for a deep cleanse of the skin.

In a cave beneath the Andes, protected and revered by locals for centuries, there is a large, heart-shaped rhodochrosite boulder that legend says is the heart of Mother Earth, which beats once every 200 years.

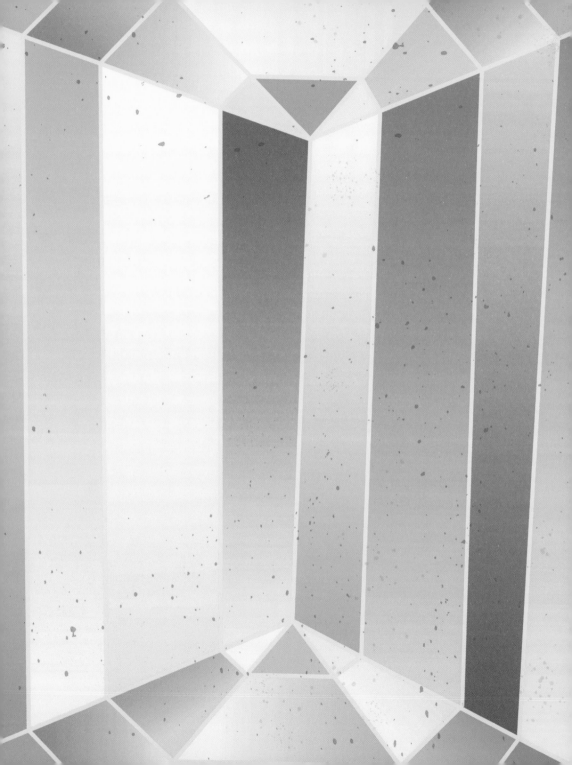

The Best Crystals For Divination

Assess the present and read the future with
a selection of carefully chosen crystals.

How to divine

Divination is the centuries-old practice of consulting the gods or goddesses—divus or diva—via tools such as runes or tarot cards to find out the best path to take, or what the outcome will be to a specific scenario. Using crystals for guidance goes back at least 5,500 years, according to the written history of early Mesopotamia—but even further back if ancient graves are anything to go by. Prehistoric people have been found buried with pouches of gems, crystal balls and polished crystal mirrors used for scrying. The ancient Greeks would use agate or jet to find out who was guilty of a crime, while Queen Elizabeth I sought the advice of her astrologer, Sir John Dee, who bought an obsidian crystal ball, with which he predicted the Spanish Armada invasion.

You can use crystal spheres, pendulums or a bag of smaller stones to help divine answers to pertinent questions.

✧ Cleanse your divination crystals before use.

✧ Whichever method you choose, first make sure to clear your mind of any worries or expectations. You need to be able to focus fully on what comes through in the present moment, and what your intuition is telling you. Tune in to your guides or a higher power for assistance if you wish.

✧ Take the time to carefully formulate the question you want to ask. Keep it as simple as possible and as close to the deeper core of what you want to know.

✧ Hold your crystals and connect with their energy. Allow them to harmonize with your energy so you can work together to get the best guidance. Ask them to show you the truth of the matter, clearly and with a timescale if necessary.

✧ Keep an open mind about the answer. Everything is possible. It might not be what it seems initially. Make a note of whatever comes to mind or is suggested by the crystal to look back at later and see if, on reflection, it makes more sense or is linked to what actually happened in some way. Take time to process your new realizations or answers, so you can make the right decision going forward.

Scrying with quartz and crystal balls

Crystal balls have long been seen as tools of personal wisdom, enabling sensitives to see into the future and make sense of the past. Scrying in crystal balls grew especially popular in 15th-century Europe, when people believed they could see angels or spirits within them to help divine the future. The most famous insight was that of Queen Elizabeth I's astrologer, Sir John Dee, who warned her of the Spanish Armada invasion after looking into an obsidian ball.

Whatever stone they are made from, all crystal spheres connect with the crown chakra and activate our psychic and clairvoyant powers, enabling us to access the Akashic records, where everything from all times—past, present and future—is recorded.

HOW TO READ A CRYSTAL SPHERE

1   First relax, ideally by candlelight, or use the light of the sun or moon to reflect into your crystal ball as you hold it.

2   Allow your energies to harmonize.

3   Ask the question you would like to have answered.

4   Sense any feelings, images or words that come to mind.

5   Place your ball down on a silk or velvet cloth.

6   Gently soften your gaze and look at your crystal sphere. It may appear to cloud over, but keep looking gently until any images appear inside the ball or in your mind. The different images may have significant meanings, or together they may make a story that serves as an answer.

7   When you've finished, disconnect from the ball and ground yourself in the present moment by taking a few deep breaths. Cover the sphere with a cloth when it's not in use.

8   Make a note of what you saw and anything you think it may represent, as well as what feelings or thoughts arose.

9   You can also do a similar reading with three smaller spheres for examining past, present and future.

10 For hidden insights into your past, or glimpses of former lives, look into an amethyst, rose quartz or calcite ball.

11 Then, to give guidance on the present connected to the past just seen, choose a sphere made of citrine or clear quartz.

12 Look into a beryl or smoky quartz crystal ball to see future opportunities or potential.

Ametrine

BEST FOR:
Concentration, connecting to spirit and angelic realms, uncovering and healing the cause of disease.

LOOKS:
Sparkling transparent stone with amethyst and citrine combined, making it shimmer shades of translucent purple and yellow.

Amethyst and citrine are naturally mixed together in this quartz crystal to make a unique combination that opens the third eye chakra, bringing deep concentration and spiritual insight for healing, meditation and divination.

In the 17th century, ametrine crystals were brought to Europe by conquistador don Felipe and given to the Queen of Spain as a thank you for letting him marry Bolivian princess Anahi of the Ayoreo tribe, whose father had given don Felipe the crystal mine as a wedding dowry. It later produced ametrine, and is still named after the princess. However, the gem didn't become popular until the 1970s and '80s.

Ametrine clears stress from the mind, so you can quickly and calmly focus during meditation. It brings higher consciousness into the physical realm, so it's good for insights and guidance that you can put into practice. It can also help lead you through astral travel, gaining wisdom while safely protected from psychic attack.

In healing and divination, ametrine gets to the bottom of things, including the root cause of diseases in the body and anxieties in the mind. Holding the stone will bring deeply hidden issues to the surface so they can be talked about and healed from. A great stone to help negotiations go smoothly and bring peace to warring sides, ametrine unifies the masculine and feminine energies within us all, and enables us to accept others more easily.

Place ametrine in your teenager's room to help them get out of bed in the morning and stay out of trouble.

Working with ametrine will enable you to contact spirit guides, angels and power animals, encouraging these higher beings to impart their wisdom and enrich our lives. Yet this stone also helps you take control of your own life with an optimistic and balanced outlook.

For a potent journey into the mind to uncover deeper truths, sit peacefully with a piece of ametrine in the light of a full moon. Imagine a door in your crystal that you can walk through into other dimensions. Visualize it in detail, seeing its shape, color and texture. Then go through that door into other realms such as the fairy forests or a portal to a past life, where you can see and bring back stories for contemplation later.

Emerald

BEST FOR:
Unconditional love, revealing the truth about relationships, stimulating clairvoyance and enhancing psychic powers.

LOOKS:
Bright green and sparkling transparent beryl.

According to legend, divine Egyptian magician Hermes engraved all the secrets of alchemy and magic on an emerald tablet. Consequently, it is believed to protect people from the illusion and enchantment of tricksters. In the Middle Ages, this much-prized gem was placed under the tongue to bring about prophetic visions of the future. Today, it is still thought to encourage clairvoyance and boost psychic skills, especially for older women.

Meditate with emerald to clear the mind and see a broader vision of life. Expect to sense a deep inner knowledge of the truth, have unconscious knowledge revealed to you, and receive the ability to discern what's right for you, along with the eloquence to express it. This calming crystal is also a useful tool for remembering past lives and the wisdom they hold for the present and future.

This green crystal of great beauty, connected to Venus, planet and goddess of love, symbolizes hope for the future, justice and security. Known as the stone of successful love, emerald promotes loyalty, unconditional love and long-lasting friendship. It is the traditional gift for anyone celebrating their 55th wedding anniversary. Wearing this gem, which activates the heart chakra, can heal relationship rifts, support mutual understanding and cooperation, and help reunite couples after a separation.

If you are counseling someone, or giving a psychic reading, use emerald to protect you from being overwhelmed with the weight of others' problems or issues. But pay attention if the emerald changes color in a reading, as this is believed to signify unfaithfulness in a relationship. Hopefully emerald's energy of renewal and harmony will encourage compassion and forgiveness, healing any heartache to appreciate what is.

Wearing an emerald will give you the strength to overcome any relationship difficulties or other trials in life, enabling you to love again with an open heart. But take it off at night, as wearing it constantly can make negative feelings rise to the surface. If this happens, however, emerald can also assist with positive reflection and renewed commitment to a higher purpose.

Iolite

BEST FOR:
Stimulating your psychic powers, creative inspiration and alternative views.

LOOKS:
Violet blue or indigo, and translucent, but becoming yellow or gray depending on the viewing angle.

A stone for enhanced vision, iolite was used by Viking explorers to help them find their way across the oceans. They used a thin piece of this color-changing crystal as the world's first polarizing lens to clear a hazy sky and enable them to see the position of the sun, even on a cloudy day, to help them accurately navigate on their travels.

Iolite stimulates the third eye, sparking clearer intuition, deep insight into your inner self and psychic awareness. It connects you to the higher realms for guidance and assists with past-life regressions. Lie down in a relaxed position holding a piece of cleansed iolite in your hand. Ask it to re-energize your aura and align your chakras. Then place iolite on your third eye to encourage a deep inner knowing and awakened consciousness. Let go of fear of the unknown and the need to control your inner experiences, and iolite will reveal the lost parts of your soul to help you move forward on your spiritual journey.

Alternatively, sit peacefully, gazing at a piece of iolite and letting its colors change as you move the stone gently in your palms. Breathe deeply and let it be your creative muse, allowing for unusual, otherworldly ideas and inspiration to come to you, and greater self-expression through the arts.

Known as the stone of witches, iolite is powerful in goddess rituals, to enhance creative spell work and increase your magical powers of manifestation. Often also used in shamanic ceremonies, the gem is good for going on an inner journey or vision quest to uncover the truth about your soul and your purpose here on earth. Pair iolite with onyx for spiritual protection and grounding, as working solely with iolite can make people feel out of their body afterwards.

Iolite helps you avoid distraction so you can focus on what is most important in work and life. In the workplace, it can encourage better brainstorming and different ways of doing things that everyone can agree on. If you are having difficulties connecting with people, it will help you see their hidden depths, or an alternative way of perceiving the problem.

Recharge iolite with natural light.

Lapis Lazuli

BEST FOR:
Prophetic dreams, increasing clairvoyance and inter-dimensional communication.

LOOKS:
Deep, royal blue flecked with gold iron pyrite pieces.

Twinkling like the night sky, lapis lazuli is made up of a mixture of stones including calcite, lazurite, sodalite and pyrite. Its celestial blue color was highly regarded by ancient civilizations, who believed it contained the power of the gods. It was used abundantly to make jewelry and as an ultramarine dye for the robes of priests and royalty. Many kings and queens of Egypt, including King Tutankhamen, had their tombs inlaid with lapis lazuli. They also wore it ground up as eyeshadow to improve their eyesight, as pictures in the Papyrus Ebers book suggest.

Lapis lazuli is a powerful stone for boosting your psychic powers. Place a piece on the third eye area in meditation and it will open up this chakra and enhance your clairvoyant and healing abilities. Meditate often with lapis and it will bring you inspired ideas in the form of visions, spiritual wisdom and intuitive guidance. Your dreams will also become rich with prophecy and meaning while working with lapis.

Lapis also balances the throat chakra, encouraging honesty and compassion in your communications, and releasing anger from past inability to speak your truth. Wearing lapis at the throat will help you face the truth of any matter with acceptance and grace, and enable you to share your opinion with others and encourage active listening, harmonizing conflict.

This stone is a strong protection talisman that stops and returns psychic attack to its sender and enlists spirit guardians to keep you safe, especially while undertaking any spiritual journeying in the mind. Meditating with it or wearing it anywhere on the body above the diaphragm will relieve stress and bring a deep sense of peace and serenity. It eases headaches, migraines and anxiety as well as calming the nervous system, and helps with any eye or ear problems. Simply hold a piece of lapis and send its healing blue light to the affected area, or place it directly on the painful spot and relax while it soothes.

If you are very attracted to lapis lazuli, you may have had a past life in any of the ancient cultures, including Atlantis or Sumeria. Use a piece of this crystal as a focus for traveling back in your mind to these past lives to see the galactic origins of humanity and communicate with beings from other dimensions.

Place lapis lazuli in your workplace to maintain integrity with your principles, inspire others' trust in you, and receive a promotion.

Onyx

BEST FOR:
Grounding, seeing the future, psychometric readings.

LOOKS:
Black with white banding or flecks like fingernails,
most often polished.

Onyx is an ancient stone that was often set in the swords and armour of warriors to promote strength and vigor in battle. It was associated with wizards and magicians due to its use in scrying and spell-work, and is still used in rituals as a grounding stone. It activates the base chakra and creates a protective shield for anyone opening up their psychic side when giving tarot-card readings, providing mediumship or spiritual counseling, for example.

Using onyx to center your energy and align you to higher guidance at the start of meditation can leave your mind free to journey into the future to see what may happen. Onyx will enhance your intuition and instinct

for what's right for you. Working with onyx encourages you to take full responsibility for your life, with confidence, stamina and strength to see you through even the toughest of times. Place a piece of onyx in your home to absorb any sadness, and stop nightmares and fear of the dark.

If someone wears onyx as jewelry, it can be used in a psychometric reading since it is believed to hold physical memories and will reveal the stories of its wearer to anyone sensitive to its energy. In healing, hold a piece of onyx, and it will guide you to a place on the body of a past-life injury. When positioned there, it will absorb the stored memory of that trauma and send universal healing energy to help.

Meditating regularly with onyx will encourage self-mastery, drive and wise decision-making. It will support you through any life changes by guiding you toward the best path for you right now. It can also help you concentrate better and keep a clear head, especially where there is conflict draining your energy.

Healing with onyx can bring you back to full health, especially if you've been working too hard or been through an illness, as it is believed to boost your immune system, cell regeneration and help your body absorb nutrients better.

Tune in to this crystal if you want to try channeling or automatic writing. As well as protecting you from unwanted energies, it will also bring you the clarity, drive and positive force needed for the highest messages to come through from spirits safely.

Recharge onyx in sunlight to boost its powers.

Red Jasper

BEST FOR:
Dowsing, nurturing ourselves and others, shamanic journeying, dream recall.

LOOKS:
Sometimes all one color from brownish, brick-red to a poppy-bright-red, or patterned with some brown or black inclusions.

Easy to carve, jasper was one of the most popular crystals to be made into seals and amulets. In Ancient Egypt, Mark Anthony had a red jasper seal ring with which he marked his letters to Cleopatra. To Native Americans, it was considered to be the sacred blood of the earth. These indigenous people found it especially helpful for tuning in to the earth to dowse for water, and many other cultures also revered jasper as a "rain bringer."

Known also as "the supreme nurturer," red jasper makes us feel whole again and want to help each other. Meditating with it feels like being wrapped in a comforting hug, perfect for grounding and relaxing you into a deep, meditative state. Hold red jasper during meditation or shamanic journeying to feel connected to and nurtured by Mother Earth. It will help you remember your dreams or imagery from any visioning, so that you can reflect on any information that may be relevant to your life at the time.

It aligns all the chakras and balances the masculine and feminine sides, bringing contentment and tranquility to all areas of your life. This alignment enhances astral travel, with each chakra's attribute playing a part in the astral journey. Place a piece of jasper on your solar plexus and heart chakra for protection before undertaking any out-of-body experience, to let it keep you safe.

Jasper brings determination and organization to projects, quick thinking and courage to tackle any problems, and honesty with yourself in all situations. In the home it will absorb negative energies including pollution and electromagnetic radiation.

Carry or wear jasper if you want to help others more, as it enables you to nurture yourself first and then share that love. This raises your awareness of your deeper needs and those of others, and the power you have to combat loneliness and isolation through reaching out. Use red jasper to increase passion in your love life, activate your imagination and help make your ideas a reality.

Jasper was used in the early history of the United States to divine the future; red jasper was used for visioning, and black jasper was thought to be good for scrying.

Ruby

BEST FOR:
Scrying, increased abundance, passion and energy.

LOOKS:
Various reds from transparent light red and raspberry to the most valuable, deep red with a blue tinge.

Shining bright red like the sun, rubies are full of our solar source's energy and vitality, which passes on to anyone wearing or working with them. Seen as more precious than even diamonds by the ancients, the Mongol Emperor Kublai Khan was said to have offered a whole city in return for a large ruby. They have always been associated with nobility and long-lasting love, representing the 40th wedding anniversary.

A powerful protector against negative energies, ruby encourages you to follow your bliss by opening the heart chakra and helping you enjoy the sensual pleasures of the physical realm. Ruby will bring passion and enthusiasm for life and love, attracting sexual partners to you by also activating the root chakra. It will increase your energy levels, motivate you to act on your goals, and fill you with a strong sense of leadership. With ruby, suppressed anger can be transmuted so you can move forward fearlessly. Thought to reflect the light of the soul, it also amplifies your innate talents and ability to succeed.

The ancients believed star ruby contains three angels or spirits to help you on your path. This variety of ruby has a six-pointed star naturally within it, on which you can focus your gaze to scry for wisdom about the past, present or future.

Sit in candlelight holding your star ruby. Look closely at the spot where the lines cross, and allow images to appear in your mind's eye or be formed on the crystal itself. These are symbols and messages from the Akashic records, where all wisdom and stories of all humanity are recorded. Sense intuitively what they mean to you. Or write them down and research their symbolism.

Many healers use star ruby, in particular, to integrate high vibrational energy into a patient's body, especially on a full moon when this gem's healing powers are even more potent. Ruby generally increases lucid dreaming, and helps you understand what you see in your dreams and decipher the meanings behind the imagery.

For an energizing meditation, lie down with ruby on your heart space. It will give your circulation, blood flow and lymphatic system a boost, increase your stamina, and fill you with dynamic life force.

Revitalize your ruby by wiping it gently with a soft cloth, then leaving it under starlight overnight.

Sapphire

BEST FOR:
Channeling wisdom and healing from higher beings, increasing psychic ability, manifestation.

LOOKS:
Sparkling, usually bright blue, but also yellow, green, violet and pink. Similar to star ruby, star sapphire has a star formation within it.

This powerful "stone of wisdom" has been the most prized of all crystals through the ages, for it brings spiritual insights, prophecy and good fortune. In ancient cultures, heavenly blue sapphire signified incredible celestial hope and faith. Buddhists believed it encouraged spiritual enlightenment, while Hindus would add sapphire to temple offerings to align astrological influences.

Initially used for spiritual healing, sapphire clears the mind and releases stress, aiding learning and understanding. It restores balance to the body and serenity to the spirit. With its ability to transform negativity of any kind, sapphire makes a powerful earth healer when used well, with enough focused intention and will during a healing session.

Sapphire can also be used to connect with the angels or source energy, possibly even extraterrestrial beings, and channel this higher consciousness for further healing of the body and mind. This power is even more amplified with healing chants, singing or music, adding gentle self-expression into the mix.

Star sapphire is believed to have the angels of faith, hope and destiny inside, known to share their knowledge with whoever gazes long enough at the intersection of lines in the pattern. Like star ruby, you can gain prophetic insight and increase your clairvoyance and clairaudience by scrying in this way with sapphire. It helps to focus your thoughts and sense the intentions of others, boosting your intuition and tuning into your own deep wisdom and truth. Working with star sapphire shows us that what we manifest is a reflection of our own essence, so keep it pure, kind and joyful.

The throat and third eye chakras are activated with blue sapphire, helping you stay self-disciplined on your spiritual path and to communicate your ideas, opinions, goals and desires clearly, and with focus, to fulfill them. Meditating regularly with this crystal assists in remembering past lives and knowing the lessons they've given you. It also assists with astral travel, so you can be transported to other places in your dream state, to bring back knowledge of all you've seen.

Sapphire releases any mental suffering or neuroses, including depression, bringing light back into your life. Its calm, balancing and healing energy encourages us into a happier life where all our dreams can come true.

Creating your own set of crystal oracle stones

You can create your own set of divination crystals easily from a selection of different colored stones. Then you can choose a few at random whenever you have a question that needs to be answered.

Start with 11 at first, one each for the main colors of black, white, brown, gray, purple, pink, red, blue, orange, yellow and green. Pick smallish crystals of around the same size, all roughly the same oval shape and tumbled so they are all smooth. Keep them in a special drawstring bag so you can easily pick them out when conducting a reading.

Settle yourself somewhere comfortable and ask your particular question or state another's issue out loud. Put your power hand (the dominant one) in the bag and choose three crystals, one at a time—or ask whoever you're giving a reading for to do the choosing. Don't look in the bag, but choose according to which ones feel right or those to which you are physically drawn. Place the crystals you've picked in front of you to figure out their meanings.

As you add more crystals to your bag, whenever you find different hues of the same color, or the right size of stones, you can then choose up to six to give you an answer to your question.

FIGURING OUT WHAT EACH CRYSTAL MEANS

Hold each crystal you've chosen, in any order, in your cupped hands to tune in to their message intuitively. Close your eyes and let images or words come to you for each crystal. Start your reading with these impressions, and then see what each stone means according to common or ancient wisdom from the list below, including most of the crystals included in this book.

DAILY SELECTION

You can also choose a crystal each morning to give you a flavor of the day ahead or guidance on what will come. Carry it with you as a good-luck charm as you go about your business.

WHAT DOES EACH GEMSTONE MEAN?

AMBER

Your hard work may finally be recognized, and success is on the way. Take time to decide how you want to use it to your very best advantage.

AMETHYST

You're going through a big life change and have experienced stress recently. Be kind and gentle to yourself until you have more energy.

AMAZONITE

Be a leader and stand up for what feels right to you. You are in a powerful position to help combat injustice.

AMETRINE

Your intuition is strong, and you can sense that you need to step in to negotiate for others or stand up for yourself.

ANGELITE

Are friends or colleagues gossiping to get one over on the other? You may be called in to arbitrate and bring peace.

AQUAMARINE

Time to broaden your horizons with new friends and travel—either physically, or in the mind through expanding your spiritual consciousness.

ARAGONITE

If you've been waiting for more luck or freedom, be patient. Unexpected help is on the way.

AZURITE

Your psychic and healing powers are getting stronger, and you may soon be able to help others with them. Let your dreams and intuition lead the way forward.

BLACK TOURMALINE

Meditate on this confusing matter more, and you will get more insight and clarity about the best solution.

BLACK OBSIDIAN

You have a lot of power at your disposal as long as you don't mind making real change. Let past upsets go as happiness is on the horizon.

BLUE CALCITE

Stay calm and keep the peace right now, even with those who provoke and are hard to tolerate.

BLUE LACE AGATE

It's time to speak your truth on the matter and see what happens. The outcome is likely to be positive.

CARNELIAN

Believe in yourself and your talents. Set your own goals and work toward them, and you will feel truly fulfilled and happy.

CELESTITE

Don't worry about what may or may not happen. This stops you from living in the present and enjoying the now—that is where the good will come.

CITRINE

Your creative talents may prove prosperous, so communicate your inspired ideas clearly. Now is the time to try some new activities that bring joy.

CLEAR QUARTZ

Time to be optimistic about your health, wealth and happiness. It's a great opportunity for new beginnings.

EMERALD

You are successful and others don't like it, but stay strong, as their jealousy will pass.

FLUORITE

Clear: You will soon have more clarity about who or what to choose to make you happy. Green: It's time to get in touch with your spiritual self by spending time around water.

GREEN AVENTURINE

Inspiration will strike you for a new lucrative endeavor. Speak up about what resources or support you need to get your idea off the ground.

HEMATITE

Make the most of the present moment and new opportunities will come your way. Don't fall into old patterns of behavior that block abundance.

IOLITE

There's more than meets the eye about that new friend or addition to the family. You can afford to go deeper with them.

JADE

Compassion is needed for anyone who is acting up. If they are being difficult to deal with, perhaps they feel inadequate, unhappy or ashamed.

JET

You need to release pain and anguish over the past, and protect yourself from any more negativity coming your way. Take time alone to do this.

LABRADORITE

Use this time to travel on your own to somewhere you've always wanted to go. It's okay to go it alone—this applies to career matters too.

LAPIS LAZULI

Rise above pettiness by sticking to your principles and what you know to be true and right for you.

MALACHITE

It could be a time for tough love. You may be feeling under pressure from others to act a certain way. Follow your heart to do what's right for you.

MOLDAVITE

If this situation makes you feel disconnected from the material world, fear not. You have a unique path to follow and special skills to share.

MOONSTONE

Are you deluding yourself about something? Or are others being deceptive? Pay attention to your dreams and listen closely to your intuition.

Index of crystals

Amber 76

Amazonite............112

Amethyst...............22

Ametrine.............138

Angelite.................24

Aquamarine........114

Aragon Star Clusters 116

Azurite 26

Black Tourmaline .28

Black Obsidian 78

Blue Calcite............30

Blue Kyanite 118

Blue Lace Agate 80

Blue Topaz 32

Carnelian.............120

Celestite.................82

Citrine 48

Clear Quartz 36

Emerald 140

Fluorite 84

Golden Topaz........50

Golden or Gold Sheen Obsidian 52

Green Aventurine 54

Green Jade 56

Hematite...............122

Iolite.....................142

Jet 86

Labradorite 38

Lapis Lazuli 144

Malachite 124

Moldavite...............40

Moonstone...........126

Moss Agate 88

Onyx.....................146

Orange Calcite 128

Peridot....................58

Pyrite 60

Red Jasper............148

Rhodochrosite.....130

Rose Quartz 62

Ruby.....................150

Sapphire...............152

Selenite 42

Shungite 90

Smokey Quartz 92

Tiger's Eye.............64

Titanium Rainbow Quartz 66

Turquoise...............94

Further reading

BOOKS

Cassandra Eason's Healing Crystals (Collins & Brown, 2003 & 2015)

The Crystal Bible by Judy Hall (Godsfield Press, 2003)

Crystal Healing Essentials by Cassandra Eason (Foulsham & Co Ltd, 2002)

Crystals, How to Use Crystal Energy to Enhance Your Life by Judy Hall (Hay House, 2015)

Crystal Prescriptions Volume 3 by Judy Hall (O Books, 2014)

The Complete Guide to Manifesting With Crystals by Marina Costello (Earthdancer, Findhorn Press, 2009)

ONLINE RESOURCES

www.crystalvaults.com

www.thecrystalcouncil.com

www.angelgrotto.com

www.kelseyaida.com

www.lonerwolf.com

www.fakeminerals.com

www.crystaltherapists.co.uk

www.thehealingchest.com

www.energymuse.com

www.healing-crystals-for-you.com

www.healingcrystals.com

www.crystalloverz.com